From Secret Track to Fast Track

From Secretary Track

to

Fast Track

The Get Ahead Guide
For Administrative Assistants,
Secretaries, Office Managers,
Receptionists, and Everyone
Who Wants More!

Ken Lizotte &
Barbara A. Litwak

amacom
American Management Association
New York • Boston • Chicago • Kansas City • San Francisco • Washington, D.C.
Brussels • Mexico City • Tokyo • Toronto

This book is available at a special
discount when ordered in bulk quantities.
For information, contact Special Sales Department,
AMACOM, a division of American Management Association,
135 West 50th Street, New York, NY 10020.

This publication is designed to provide accurate and authoritative
information in regard to the subject matter covered. It is sold with the
understanding that the publisher is not engaged in rendering legal,
accounting, or other professional service. If legal advice or other expert
assistance is required, the services of a competent professional person
should be sought.

Library of Congress Cataloging-in-Publication Data

Lizotte, Ken.
    From secretary track to fast track / Ken Lizotte & Barbara A.
Litwak.
        p.   cm.
    "The get ahead guide for administrative assistants, secretaries,
office managers, receptionists, ..."
    Includes bibliographical references and index.
    ISBN 0-8144-7902-2 (pbk.)
    1. Secretaries—Vocational guidance.   2. Receptionists—Vocational
guidance.   3. Career development.   I. Litwak, Barbara A.
II. Title.
HF5547.5.L59   1996
651.3'74'02373—dc20
[B]   96-2128
                                                                   CIP

Printing number

10   9   8   7   6   5   4   3   2   1

To Christie, office manager and poetess extraordinaire
—K.L.

To all admins—who've been there and back
—B.A.L.

Contents

Acknowledgments

Contrary to myth, most books spring forth not from isolated so-journs in ivory towers but from nitty-gritty collaborations with thoughtful, generous supporters who give of themselves, their ideas, and their time for the simple good of the project. We'd like to offer all such supporters a rousing round of acknowledgment. We're sincere when we say we could in no way have accomplished this book without you.

We'd first like to acknowledge those admins and ex-admins who are graduates of our CareerScape® programs: Angela Maffeo, Carol McDonough, Anne Marie Dangler, Cary Schwartz, Mary Miller, and Judy Tyler. We appreciate your continued enthusiasm for the work we do.

Thanks also to those heroic ex-admins who agreed to share with us their stories: Sophia Snow, Judy Wagner, Jessica Lefcourt, Sharon Casey, Kristina Cavanaugh, Gwen Champion, Janet Hartford-Hill, Marg Balcom, Nancy Cassesso, Rusty Stieff, Chantal Weaver, and Marsha Miller.

Acknowledgments too to experts Paul Falcone and Ethel Cook for sharing their professional observations, and to Cheri Ditsch at Professional Secretaries International for providing PSI's official history of the secretarial profession. Also, thank you Louise Bonar, Martin Duffy, and Catherine Radigund for your research ideas.

To the staff at Katharine Gibbs Schools: We appreciated your opening up to us as we probed background information for this book. Kudos especially to Vicki Valhouli for a wonderful, instructive, impromptu tour of the Boston school and to the incomparable Susan Max in New York, who unearthed valuable historical materials on Katy herself when no one else even knew where to look.

Finally, our heartiest acknowledgment goes to the insightful, delightful Mary Glenn, our editor, whose steady commanding of this project and unwavering belief in us and our ideas spurred us forward a thousand extra miles. Mary, this book is so much the better because of thee!

Prologue

Something's been grumbling inside you for a long time. It's not your stomach (you just ate!), so you're hard-pressed to know exactly what's going on. Yet each day that goes by, especially each workday, its impact on you becomes harder to deny. This grumbling, this gnawing ache has been gathering steam for a while now, and you've tried everything you can think of to relieve it.

"Maybe I just need a vacation," you said to yourself once upon a time. Then you took off on a great one, flew to the Virgin Islands, lolled on the beaches, went scuba diving, and consumed many fabulous meals, while the sun set over the brilliant turquoise Caribbean waters—and still that grumbling throbbed inside you the whole time. Ten days later you returned to your desk, seemingly refreshed. But the ache hadn't gone away.

Lately you've been gazing in wonder at your colleagues around your office and thinking, "What's wrong with me?" Everyone else around you acts so contented. They all seem very happy. They come in in the morning, go about their work, finish up their projects, head on home. No apparent problems. Why can't *you* feel like that?

How's Your Career Health?

Excuse us for a moment: May we play doctor now? We'd like to examine your "career health," if you don't mind; see if there's medicine to prescribe. We'll do our best to come up with an accurate diagnosis. Would you mind filling out a few insurance forms before we get started?

Seriously, if you've been flirting with any of the disgruntled feelings described here, take heart: You're normal! What's more, you know all those "contented" colleagues you see around you, those peaceful working folk you wish you could be a little more like? Well, guess what? You're probably more like them than you realize. Why, we wouldn't be a bit surprised if they all felt exactly the way you do. They probably think *you're* the most tranquil, contented colleague in the whole place.

Everyone experiences dissatisfaction about their work from time to time, and often that really does mean that a good vacation is indeed what's called for. A little breathing space, a change of scenery. Sometimes that's really all it is. Once you've satisfied an urge to temporarily get away, your life and work return to normal.

Other times, though, it's more than that. When a "grumbling" keeps nagging at you, day after day, month after month, year after year, then things have gotten serious. If you stay in your present situation and deny this inner ache, you risk mental, physical, and emotional ill health. Left to themselves, unsettling conditions in our work lives rarely improve.

We can explore this further by giving you a checkup. Please answer each of the following questions as honestly as possible. Since they're all very general, just check off a response that seems closest to the truth. Your doctors (us) will return in a minute.

	Yes	No
Have you been sleeping well?	_____	_____
Does your work challenge you?	_____	_____
Do you enjoy the people you work with?	_____	_____
Do you make enough money?	_____	_____
Do you feel well treated by your boss?	_____	_____
Do you only occasionally leave work feeling taken advantage of?	_____	_____
Do you only occasionally leave work feeling emotionally drained?	_____	_____
Can you identify genuine advancement opportunities where you work?	_____	_____

Do you find your work meaningful? _____ _____
Can you see yourself in this job five years from
   now? _____ _____
Do you feel you are growing as a person as a
   result of your current job? _____ _____
Do you look forward to going to work in the
   mornings? _____ _____
Do you look forward to Monday mornings? _____ _____
Do you feel that your best talents are being
   utilized? _____ _____
Do you feel that you're listened to at work? _____ _____
Do you feel that you're given sufficient credit
   for the good things you do at this job? _____ _____

How did you do? Did you check more yeses or more noes? If you checked more noes, we'll have to level with you: You've contracted a serious case of "admin's disease." Yes, that's correct—you're not well.

But serious career illness can't be cured with vacations, weekends, a slight change in work assignments, or a dose of aspirin or penicillin. You're telling yourself with all these noes—let's say five or more—that you've just got to move on. Moving on to what, of course, may be the $64-trillion question, but move on you must.

So let's do it!

From Secretary Track

to

Fast Track

Introduction

Watching Our Language

During early research on this book, we asked Carol McDonough, one of the great executive administrative assistants working today, how she defined her profession. Carol answered without hesitation: "I'm a nanny for big people," she snapped, both twinkling and hinting at exasperation in the same breath. To administrative assistants, admins, secretaries, receptionists, office managers, file clerks, and all the myriad other terms that represent those who toil away in the "pink-collar ghetto," we could now add perhaps the most descriptive (and accurate) of all—*nanny*.

There are indeed lots of ways to describe what administrative personnel do in their day-to-day exertions to support bosses, managers, supervisors, presidents, CEOs, and owners (not to mention colleagues, vendors, and clientele). It's a vast, hard-to-pin-down role, shifting with the sands of time, need, urgency, and, just as frequently, a boss's mood. It's also a role that's begun changing more than ever, which is why agreeing upon one common label for a job with so many variations becomes all the more tricky.

So allow us to settle the matter. In this book, we use two terms interchangeably: *administrative assistant* and *admin*. When using these terms, we embrace everyone who works in any kind of "support" capacity, including secretaries, receptionists, office managers, file clerks, mail-room assistants, switchboard operators. Since *administrative assistant* can be applied to each of these professionals in one form or another, unlike the more traditional, better-known category of secretary, and since *administrative assistant* has evolved into a title many feel offers more respect, we'll stick with it.

We can't use these terms exclusively, however, since the term *secretary* as a title hasn't completely died in our language—nor should it. While many admins would love to deep-six this term, conveying, they say, the stereotypical image of a ditsy, dictation-taking, gum-popping, typewriting servant girl, the fact is, there's still a place for it. For one thing, many admins identify themselves as secretaries (or as having once been secretaries) and see the secretarial role as a positive, specialized one that business could never do without.

For another, retaining the term *secretary* in our language still feels natural to many admins. It doesn't seem right to them to call themselves anything else. So we'll use *secretary* whenever appropriate to our discussions and substitute *admin* everywhere else. Though language changes over time, it's generally a long time. We can wait.

While on the matter of explaining our choice of language, we might also elaborate on a couple of more terms. The term *pink collar* sprang up during the 1960s and 1970s to describe administrative support professionals in general. Because so many were (and still are) women, the color pink was chosen (get it?). To include admins among the "blue collars" obviously wouldn't work, since *blue collar* refers to factory workers (and other forms of hands-on labor), while *white collar*, though that's how admins had been originally labeled, refers to the mostly male ranks of office workers with authority—managers, technical decision makers, financial experts. The growth in the numbers of admins in the business world since World War II, then, begged for a new name.

We'll also use, most times, the pronouns *she* and *her* to refer to admins, and *he* and *him* to refer to bosses and supervisors. We do this not out of misguided Neanderthal sexist leanings or as a convenient grammatical device to make our work easier. Instead we want our examination of career issues for admins to take on a real-life flavor.

The unfortunate reality of today's work world confronts us with unsettling facts: While 95 percent of pink-collar professionals are women, 97 percent of senior-level managers are men. Though more and more women rise to management status every year, and though over half of today's workforce is female, admins must still remember that personal career victories will rarely be won easily. A commitment to change only begins the process, while fighting against the odds could absorb 99 percent of the rest. So know what you're up against by keeping your focus on real-world conditions. In that way, we'll best prepare you to win.

You *can* escape the pink-collar ghetto. You *can* forge a career life that's exactly the way you want it. So listen to the lessons, insights, advice, and wisdom you'll find in the admin success stories we report in this book. Then go out and apply them to the obstacles in your path. Every admin mentioned or profiled here has a bit of career advancement wisdom to impart. Be sure you savor every morsel.

1

Trapped in the Pink-Collar Ghetto

Shall we start off with a little quiz? Don't panic; there's no cause for alarm. Just think of this as a warm-up. We're going to be looking at your life as an admin from every perspective imaginable, so we thought we might begin by clarifying what an admin (like you) really does.

Sometimes we take our reality for granted, especially when things get negative or unsatisfying. You probably picked up this book because you're feeling ready to move on, in some way or other. We'll assume that staying where you are will likely lead to big feelings of stagnation and meaninglessness about your work (or your life), if it hasn't already. In that frame of mind, then, it would be easy to dismiss everything you've accomplished or currently do, as if they have no value in the marketplace.

Of course, you would be wrong.

So, as we begin our adventure, let's consider what admins really do: How do you operate? Whom do you work for? What do you have to deal with? What do you routinely achieve?

Evaluate each of the three following scenes on the basis of your personal knowledge and experiences as an admin. Which scenes seem real to you? Which sound made up or improbable? When you've finished evaluating all three, we'll explore the implications of your thoughts.

Scene 1

Marta feels like a sitting duck. From her desk, she can see all six of her bosses' offices at once. What's more, each can see her as soon as he walks out of his office. That means that no sooner does one boss drop a file on her desk for her to type than a second comes hustling out her way with a long list of phone calls for her to make.

And when does all this need to be done? ASAP, of course!

You can imagine the rest. Marta wishes that boss number one had hung around long enough to tell her if he wanted his document typed on letterhead or entered into the computer (or both), and whether he needed just one copy for himself or wanted her to distribute it to someone else in the company. "Questions, questions," she sighs.

Then she looks at boss number two's list of names and phone numbers. "OK," she thinks, "I'll call them." Only question here is, "What am I calling to tell them?" But boss number two is long gone to an appointment out of the building.

The job's only saving grace is boss number three. Of the six male managers Marta reports to, he's the only one who regularly greets her by name and asks politely if she has time to do this task or that. He even waits around to answer any questions she may have about what he wants her to do.

And—get this—whenever she does anything at all for him, really truly anything, he flashes a boyish though quite genuine grin and leaves her with an enthusiastic "Splendid!"

Rating: On a scale of 1 (least) to 10 (most), how real does this scene seem to you?

Your rating: [   ]

How does it invoke your own experience as an admin? Have you ever heard of a similar scene from any of your admin colleagues? Have you ever had a job like this? Make a few notes here summarizing your thoughts:

_____

_____

_____

_____

_____

Scene 2

Eva likens her days as an admin for a large insurance company to a comic strip she once saw: One character is peering over the top of his cubicle trying to get the attention of another character three cubicles down. Once he does, he asks, "Hey, are you new around here?" Then: "Whatcha in for?"

Eva knows the feeling. Working at that insurance company had felt like a prison sentence too. They'd crammed her inside a tight, poorly lit, gray cubicle and instructed her to collate and staple insurance forms all day. One after another, hour after mind-numbing hour, Eva checked off in red pencil a little box at the top of page 1 of each set (to indicate that she'd handled and stapled the set). Then she filled cardboard boxes with the completed sets and filed the contents twice each day somewhere within a high, wide bank of pale green file cabinets at the end of a long corridor bordered by more tight, gray cubicles with admins inside doing just what she was doing.

"Whatcha in for?" indeed! She remembers staying sane only by constantly daydreaming about how to break out.

Rating: On a scale of 1 (least) to 10 (most), how real does this scene seem to you?

Your rating: [   ]

How does it invoke your own experience as an admin? Have you ever heard of a similar scene from any of your admin colleagues? Have you ever had a job like this? Make a few notes here summarizing your thoughts:

_____

_____

_____

_____

_____

SCENE 3

When interviewing for a position as an executive secretary, Gwen finds herself a little bewildered. The man interviewing her appears unusually . . . well, "human"! For more than nine years she's worked for four other managers, none of whom, except on the rarest of days, have ever acted as if they cared one whit about how she was doing. But this man seems different.

"How do you see yourself doing this job?" he asks. "How have you handled similar jobs [or similar tasks] in the past? What kind of resources might you need to do your work well here? How might I assist you?"

There are more personalized professional questions too: "How do you see your future? Tell me about your professional goals. How could working here advance you along your career path?"

This prospective employer seems impressed that she has an MBA and is not at all concerned that she may be overqualified. "I prefer working with someone who wants to move up the ladder," he explains. "Your MBA shows that you've got goals for yourself, that you take pride in your work. When we think that way, we realize that only by doing a super job will we advance to the next step."

Gwen can't believe this. He wants to be both a boss and a mentor? There must be a catch. Her confusion continues when he points to his Rolodex and says, "Any name and phone number you find in there is yours."

Gwen's fears, however, prove groundless. Three months into the new job, she sees that her new boss means exactly what he said during her job interview. With his help and his blessing, she moves on to a higher position in the organization within the year.

Rating: On a scale of 1 (least) to 10 (most), how real does this scene seem to you?

Your rating: [   ]

How does it invoke your own experience as an admin? Have you ever heard of a similar scene from any of your admin colleagues? Have you ever had an experience like this? Make a few notes on the next page summarizing your thoughts:

_____

_____

_____

_____
                        *
_____

And now for some answers. Did you guess that Marta's scene was a real one? If you did, you guessed right! Did you feel that Eva's scene could really happen? Right again! How about Gwen's experience? No way, right? How could a boss be so supportive? But maybe you actually *have* encountered someone like this, in which case you may have rated Scene 3 as a probable scenario. If so, you guessed correctly once again!

All three of these scenes actually happened. How do we know? Can we prove it, you ask skeptically. Yes, we certainly can because all three happened to one of your faithful co-authors, Barbara A. Litwak.

In Barbara's own words:

> "Being an admin can run the gamut, from the worst, bottom-of-the-barrel type experience to one that brings you great respect and satisfaction. Much depends on whom you work for. Even more, though, may depend on your self-image. Do you believe that you can have what you want in life, that it's OK, that it's possible? I saw lots of admins along the way who held themselves back by not setting goals and acting on them. Once I found a boss who was willing to be my mentor, I was on my way. But only because I'd prepared for him."

Can you use your experience as an administrative assistant to guide you to bigger and better things? Can you use admin work as a springboard for getting a new career off the ground? Can you actually locate a boss who will really help you advance your goals?

Barbara did. Many other admins we've spoken to during our research for this book have done it too. Many of the admins

that have come to the career seminars we've hosted over the
years have done it as well. And many, many more stories we
come across in the media or in casual conversation prove it's
possible for you also.

Though your boss and others at your place of work may
want to look upon you as "just an admin" or "just a secretary,"
and even if people keep advising you to forget about advancing,
that you've landed in the final station of your professional work
life and that you might as well accept it, you're going to be hearing very different messages here. And the good news is, we
know what we're talking about.

We can always change anything that's happening in our
lives because we come into this world as powerful, talented,
fully creative human beings. Now we're not just saying this to
throw in a little touchy-feely here or to kiss up to you just because you've plunked down a few dollars for this book! Uh-
uh, we're saying it because it's true. In fact, the only difference
between you and the admins you'll find profiled in this book is
this: Despite suffering many of the emotions you probably feel
now—fear, doubts, frustrations, confusion—they stayed with
the fight long enough to attain their dreams.

Maybe you're just getting started in this process. Or maybe
you've been working on your career advancement for a while
and you've recently been feeling discouraged. Maybe you've
slowed down a bit, lost some momentum. You may even have
told someone something like, "I'm never going to get out of this
job; it's too hard. Nobody wants me because all I know is administrative work. I'm trapped here."

We hope that whoever listened to your drivel cared about
you enough to retort, "Stop whining, willya? You can be anything you darn well want to be. Just dust yourself off and keep
goin'. There's gold in them thar' hills!"

All too often, however, that's not what we hear. (Who says
"thar' " these days, anyway?) More likely, your friend or spouse
complied a little too quickly and a tad too obsequiously with
your sentiments, muttering something like, "Well, you're probably right. It really is hard to make a move these days. Maybe you
ought to just stay where you are. Things might get better some
day."

Well, as we've said, you won't hear that sort of thing from us. Instead let's work together here to guide you to higher levels of both your career life and day-to-day attitudes in your personal life. We'll lead you through a process that can keep you fresh, vibrant, and constantly in tune with your wants and needs. You'll become more confident than ever before, and you'll never again need to return to your present life as an administrative assistant unless you want to. From this point on, your career becomes a function of your personal choices.

Starting Point: R-E-S-P-E-C-T

It's easy to fall into the pink-collar trap that society has set for you. This trap has been consolidating its strength for a long, long time. You may have innocently set your foot inside it some time in your past, and since then its clamps have slammed shut.

What's the pink-collar trap? Just that the great work you do doesn't need to be even acknowledged because just *anybody* could do it, after all. You admins are really nothing special—you're dispensable, far less valuable than everyone around you. You can be replaced, in a heartbeat. In the words of Rodney Dangerfield, you quite simply "don't get no respect."

But respect *is* a necessity, especially if you're planning to turn yourself inside out and make a major career move. Otherwise, you begin believing that (1) you don't deserve a fabulous career life, and (2) the knowledge and expertise you've developed during your admin years aren't all that special. You then start devaluing yourself and disbelieving you can ever make such a change. And that only buys you a one-way ticket to Nowheresville.

Interestingly, the historical facts surrounding the admin profession suggest other scenarios. Admin/secretarial work originally enjoyed the highest levels of respect and prestige in the heady early days of the profession when mostly men worked as admins. Not until women began populating the majority of admin situations did societal attitudes toward the profession shift downward. Only then did the profession become treated as something just about anyone could do. Surprised? Us neither.

Let's step into a time machine for a moment and take a look at how this all came about. You may find it instructive to learn that there's a much larger dynamic swirling about you than simply individuals' attitudes toward you personally. By sizing up the subtle adversities you've been expected to endure, you may recognize that you've got a lot more going for you than even many higher-paid, better-respected (mostly male) coworkers.

Mommy, Where Do Admins Come From?

Did you know that in Africa there exists an elegant, long-legged white bird with magnificent, flowery plumage that spends its days strutting about grasslands and meadows while patiently searching out its prey? Did you know that this sleek, agile, exotic bird can ward off annoying irritants (snakes, small birds, flying insects) with quick, expert flicks of its wings? "Hmmm, very interesting, Ken and Barbara," we hear you saying, "but what the heck's all this got to do with *me*?"

Only that this bird has long, elegant crest feathers that stick out from the back of its head, and reminded nineteenth-century explorers of the office clerks and personal secretaries they knew back in Merry Old England who used to absentmindedly poke quill pens behind their ears as they searched for another kind of prey—documents, files, letters. And these earliest administrative assistants also became adept at waving off irritants—the many unwanted visitors and solicitors seeking audiences with their busy masters. *Flick, flip*—the admin's authoritative hands and arms shooed them away. "Be gone with you now! Master can't see you."

It was natural, then, for these English explorers to dub this determined, skillful, and exquisite jungle fowl the "secretary bird."

To us, a good admin parallels the African secretary bird in a couple of other significant ways as well. No matter what conditions you encounter as you begin your workday, whether it's six bosses tossing documents at you simultaneously or irritating intruders slithering into or fluttering about your reception lobby, you probably routinely handle it all with the same patient, competent grace as the secretary bird.

And, it's a good bet the world pays your excellent work little notice. Had *you*, for example, ever heard of the secretary bird before? We hadn't. But think about it: It's been out there on the African plains all along, quietly taking care of business. And with an air of professionalism and bearing second to none.

Yet the profession hasn't always been thus ignored. Back when mostly men served as admins, society paid much more attention. In fact, early male admins and secretaries drew not only other folks' respect but their envy. It was a good, clean job that got one out of the factory, and it required a certain intelligence and education (much reading, writing, and arithmetic). Compared to today's wages, an admin's salary was pretty good too—a man could actually raise a family doing this job! We'd guess all this translated into far sturdier self-images than most admins harbor today.

The word *secretary* itself derives originally from the Latin *secretum*, meaning "secret." The earliest secretaries and administrative assistants, true confidants to their bosses, recorded or observed all a master's thoughts, wisdom, needs, and desires. "As affairs of commerce and trade expanded," notes Professional Secretaries International (PSI), the Association for Office Professionals™, in its official history of the admin profession (published in *The Secretary* magazine), "men of wealth and power had need of secretaries (confidants or trusted agents) to kings and other rulers, as they handled their correspondence on private or secret matters, particularly matters of state." Translation: It was a pretty important and high-class job!

Throughout the ages, secretaries and administrative assistants have shown up everywhere—at the right arms of emperors in Rome, kings and queens of the Renaissance, ministers and presidents today. But it was the rise of expanding industries and worldwide commerce that really spawned the widespread need for admins. Not until then did dutiful record-keeping and regular business correspondence become such a critical business function for everyone.

From White to Pink

In the late nineteenth century, however, the profession of administrative assistance began falling from grace. As long as men held these positions, people thought of professional admins as smart, clever individuals who had escaped the grunge and rigors of factory or farm work via their obviously superior intellects. When women entered the ranks, however, the admin pedestal toppled over.

With urban industrial society expanding at a steady clip, more and more management slots opened up, which only experienced male admin "white collars" seemed qualified to fill. How then to fill the many newly vacant admin slots? Only one solution looked practical: Unlock the kitchen doors and let out the women. To maintain the balance of power between the sexes (and to keep expenses down!), this of course might mean redefining the value of the work itself. But the work had to be done by someone: That much was clear.

At the same time, new mechanical inventions introduced an added wrinkle, specifically in the form of Remington's first "writing machine." Indeed, the sight of ten, twenty, fifty professional "type writers," as the women themselves were initially called, sitting at small desks lined up neatly in big factory-like office rooms and clacking away on these strange, black, bulky new machines must have sealed the admin's doom. Admin mass production had arrived, and every face was female. The job no longer seemed so special.

"As women entered offices to perform the once coveted role of secretary," the PSI historical sheet explains, "it became one of growing disdain. They labored the same long hours as men—at considerably less pay. Few received recognition and promotion. [This] mass endured a role of servitude with loyalty, while perfecting their shorthand, transcription and typing skills."

The Katy Gibbs Revolution

By 1900 the once male-only bastion of administrative assistance had become the domain of women. Business schools teaching the secretarial "arts" had sprung up around the country, many with "for women" attached to their principal title. Demand grew. So many companies clamored for trained, knowledgeable "type-writing girls" that despite its newly subservient status, the job had become an indispensable component of the industrial organizational "machine."

About the same time, Katharine Gibbs, a Rhode Island widow struggling to find ways to feed her children, got an idea. Why not start a business college for women that emphasized not only business skills like typing and dictation but also polished professional attitudes? Wouldn't personal assistants and secretaries increase their value to employers if they projected sophisticated communication skills and fine manners? Accomplishing that, mightn't the "type-writing girl" then be elevated to true professional status via her obvious commitment to work excellence and pride in herself?

In 1911, Mrs. Gibbs opened the first door to her "business finishing school" for women in Providence. Her idea apparently fit the times because the next few years would see her open branches of her college in New York City and Boston. The Katharine Gibbs School today (or "Katy Gibbs," as its graduates affectionately call it) now operates in seven locations on the East Coast and is perhaps the country's best-known, short-term secretarial school.

Out With the Old, In With the New

Katy Gibbs introduced into the newly evolving structures of the business world an opportunity for the legions of "type-writing girls" to enjoy individual recognition and dignity. No longer did the administrative assistants of her day need to see themselves as faceless handmaidens or as human versions of machines. They could now emerge from obscurity with smarter ways of doing things, a genuine desire to help their employers grow, and a loyalty toward getting the job done no matter what. In short, no longer did any woman have to consider herself "only a secretary."

But old ideas die hard. Today, though more and more admins insist on calling themselves (and being called) administrative assistants (as opposed to secretaries or clerks), many still retain low professional self-images. The sense of laboring in a pink-collar ghetto leaves many admins with a dispiriting sense that the only way out is through either marriage or retirement. The barriers are too formidable, high, and impenetrable.

Fortunately, the facts do not support cries of doom and despondence. There really are lots of options. The key to knowing this lies in your attitude.

Attitude Exam

Time for another quiz, everyone! This time we're going to gauge the awesome powers of your "attitude." As in: What do you believe about your chances for success? How do you perceive your potential? What kind of credit do you give yourself?

Let's start by surveying typical laments often uttered by your colleagues. These laments are composites of the many, many we have heard in our career programs throughout the years. What do you notice about them? Do you recognize any common themes?

Think about how you might respond to each lament should the lamenter beg you for an answer. What advice would you give? Would you take (and utilize) this same advice yourself?

Wilma: "I'm only a secretary, see? They call me an administrative assistant, but I'm not. I'm a secretary. What else can I do, anyway? It's all I know."

Corinne: "I once applied for another job inside the company. When my boss heard about it, he hit the roof. 'How could you do this to me?' he said. 'You know how much I need you here!' I felt awful."

Bobbi: "Whenever I go out with my friends who are also admins, all they want to talk about is men, parties, outfits. I'd really like to move up in this company and do something else, like work in marketing or sales, but I just don't know how. None of my friends have any ambitions."

Edna: "I asked personnel if they could help me find a position with more responsibility and challenge. They gave me a skills inventory test and you know what it showed? My skills and experience qualify me for exactly what I do now— answering the phones, greeting visitors, and typing. That's all I am! The personnel director told me if I wanted to qualify for something else I'd have to go back to school. Well, I don't know if I *want* to go back to school."

What did you notice? Did you catch any themes? How would you react to any of these statements if they were brought to you? What actions would you suggest? What attitudes do you feel need to change?

On the lines below, jot down a few of your reactions to these laments. Include advice you'd give each lamenter. After you're done, we'll let you see ours. But don't look ahead to check out our "right" answers. We're not your teacher here as much as your guide. There really aren't any "right" answers. We're just exploring as many avenues as we can to extract you from the pink-collar ghetto. There are many, many ways to do it.

Response to Wilma: "_____

_____

_____

_____

_____."

Response to Corinne: "_____

_____

_____

_____

_____."

Response to Bobbi: "_____

_____

_____

_____

_____."

Response to Edna: "_____

_____

_____

_____."

Reactions From the Home Office

Too many admins sit themselves down inside boxes of their own construction and refuse to climb out. Though it often seems logical to suppose that you're trapped in a professional role because of skills and experience, in our experience it's *never* so. Why, we've met grown men and women of every professional stripe who succumb to what we call "self-entrapment," though in admins, because of the subtle discouragements we've talked about, negative self-beliefs often run deepest of all.

Our general reaction to these statements is this: *Stop whining!* It was, after all, your choice that brought you to admin work in the first place. It will be your choice (or a series of choices) that will get you away from it. So stop acting as if life were impossible.

One theme that runs through all these statements is helplessness. Wilma is "only" a secretary and she can't do anything about it. Corinne can never move on because her boss doesn't approve. Bobbi's friends have no ambition and won't let her talk about things that matter to her. Edna has no skills that qualify her for any other kind of work. Everyone seems to be paraphrasing a well-known line of Oliver Hardy's: "Why won't someone do something to help me?"

Our suggestion? Admin, help thyself! That's it in a nutshell, and once again it comes back to our old friend *attitude*. If you can conceive it and you believe it, you can achieve it. It's got to start with you, though, right inside your little ol' head.

Our Specific Prescriptions

Here's how we would react to these admins' laments:

Response to Wilma: "By calling you an administrative assistant and not a secretary, they're giving you an opening. Wilma, this is a beginning, a chance to define yourself as something more. Take it, take it! However, rather than wait for others to flesh out a new job description, start thinking about what you'd like to do yourself. What projects would you like to tackle? What skills would you like to add to your repertoire?

"By restructuring your job definition (and skill set), you'll initiate a personal assessment of your interests and set new professional goals."

Response to Corinne: "Understand this—your responsibility in life can never be to subvert your own interests to your current boss's approval (or disapproval). So what if he doesn't like the idea of your moving on? He'll get over it!

"While it would have been helpful to get his approval for strategic reasons, it may be too late now. So go on without him; don't give up on your plans. Start laying the groundwork for someone to replace you. You might try to explain to him your need to move on, but if he won't listen just keep making contacts and looking for other openings. You may have to look outside your company, it's true, but whatever you do, keep looking!

"In the end, everybody (including your boss) will be the happier for it."

Response to Bobbi: "When you're out with your friends and colleagues, inject topics of interest to *you* into the conversation. Insist on equal time. If that doesn't work, it's time to go and find some new friends.

"You chose the friends you now have once upon a time and you can unchoose them if the reasons for having them in your life have passed. If they're no longer meeting your needs, or you want to add new colleagues and friends that better meet your interests and needs, go to it! There's no excuse for staying bored and stagnant."

Response to Edna: "OK, maybe you really don't want to go back to school right now, but that may be because you haven't developed the passion to do so. Forget what those tests tell you. Just answer this one question: What do you want to do with the next phase of your work life? Yes, that's the question: What do you *want*?

"Many of the skills you use today can be transferred to other jobs, other careers, other employers. Maybe you even want to go into business for yourself. What work do you see others doing that looks like fun? Start making a list and asking yourself what skills these folks employ that you also utilize in your work. Something like that could open your eyes."

Help Is on the Way

By picking up this book and starting to read it, you've made yourself a career commitment. You've decided to change your life. Whether you've been fantasizing about getting promoted, moving laterally to a new department, changing your career, quitting your present job—whatever!—something inside you has begun counseling you that you can do it.

We've talked a lot about attitudes in this first chapter. While it's true that external forces will throw troubling obstacles in the way of our hopes and dreams, know also that only your own inner barriers can truly stand in your way. Overcome these barriers and nothing can stop you. Like our friend the African secretary bird, keep on searching, searching, searching for what you want while flicking away irritants with a wave of your wing.

How Confident Are You?

Have you been letting too many inner barriers stand in the way of your success? Do you tend to yield too much power to external forces? Do you delay personal career victory by living off excuses?

In the accompanying worksheet, let's take a readout of your "positive self-belief"—that is, your level of self-confidence about your chances for true career advancement.

Please score the following statements using the scale below:

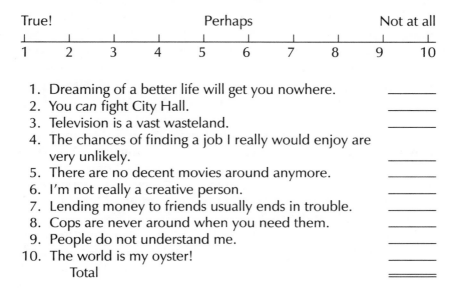

True!				Perhaps				Not at all
1	2	3	4	5	6	7	8	9	10

1. Dreaming of a better life will get you nowhere. _____
2. You *can* fight City Hall. _____
3. Television is a vast wasteland. _____
4. The chances of finding a job I really would enjoy are very unlikely. _____
5. There are no decent movies around anymore. _____
6. I'm not really a creative person. _____
7. Lending money to friends usually ends in trouble. _____
8. Cops are never around when you need them. _____
9. People do not understand me. _____
10. The world is my oyster! _____
   Total _____

Scoring: Give yourself two points if you marked an 8 or higher on questions 1, 3, 4, 5, 6, 7, 8, and 9, one point if you marked a 4, 5, 6, or 7 on these questions, and no points if you marked a 3 or lower.

Give yourself two points if you marked a 3 or lower on questions 2 and 10, one point if you marked a 4, 5, 6, or 7 on these questions, and no points if you marked an 8 or higher.

Now total all your scores.

How did you do? Did you score 20? If so, you scored *big*! That's a perfect score, and it means you absolutely, no-question-about-it, couldn't be more of a positive thinker if you tried. You're optimistic, you believe in your ability to effect change, and you've got your barriers in check or you're constantly working on them. It's unlikely that you let yourself feel victimized for any great length of time.

Note of caution: Does this mean that you never have to work on your barriers, that everything comes easy to you? Probably not. More likely you have to work on your inner barriers the same as everyone else. But you probably give yourself effective inner signals to make your efforts at eradicating your barriers pay off. You've decided in your head that you can do it.

If you scored 15 to 19, you're on your way to heaven, although you're not quite there yet. You probably know that you've got to keep watch on yourself so you don't stray from the path. We suggest periodically asking yourself these questions: Which inner barriers do I most want to get rid of? Which give me the most trouble? What solutions can I think of to keep them in check?

A score of 8 to 14 means you have some work to do. There may be a bug in your ear that keeps whispering something like this: "No matter what you do, you can probably never make it. You've got too much going against you. What in tarnation ever made you think you could better your life anyway? Forget about all this, OK? It's not in the cards."

For you, it's time to set free that wild, never-say-die secretary bird that lives inside you! Go find what you want and flick away all the naysaying that gets in your way. Put this book down for a moment and begin flapping those powerful, elegant secretary bird wings. Go ahead, do what we tell you. We'll wait. (*Flap, flap, flap.*)

Now then, didn't that feel wonderful? Practice your wing flapping throughout each and every day. Practice it especially at work. It will make you stronger.

Did we leave anybody out? Oh, you say you scored less than 8? Well, then, you've got a *lot* of work to do! But fear not; you won't be going this hard road alone. After all, you did buy this book!

Trust us when we tell you this, and this goes for everyone: You've got greatness inside of you, and you're about to display it. You're embarking on a great adventure that will take you to a brave new world.

FROM THE ADMIN FILES

Name of ex-admin: Judy Tyler

Currently: Advertising account executive for *Premier Bride* magazine, selling ad space, establishing and managing distribution, and implementing marketing services for client advertisers

Admin skills used today: Meeting planning, management and leadership, and people and telephone skills

How change was made: "Something inside me always told me I wanted to be in marketing and sales. I used to see other people in the companies I worked in traveling and making decisions, and I'd think, 'I can do that.'

"So I went back to school for a marketing degree. Then I found a mentor who encouraged me to keep studying and to look for opportunities that mattered to me. About the time I finished my bachelor's, I got hired to my first non-admin position, as a print specialist in production at a large high-tech firm. From there I went on to marketing and management positions."

Best advice for admins: "Visibility is a key thing. Take advantage of every opportunity to get as much out front as you can. Vendors and customers you've worked with are fabulous networking opportunities. Chairing meetings and getting involved in committees let people get to know how good you are.

"Also, go back to school! After I finished my bachelor's, I proudly announced to my mentor that I had just taken my last exam, that I was finally done. He congratulated me, but added, 'Judy, don't stop now. Your bachelor's is something you have to have, but a master's degree will open doors for you.' I couldn't see it then, but gradually it sank in. Three years later I had earned a master's degree in applied management."

2

External Forces, Inner Barriers

There's a scene in the movie *Working Girl* in which the Melanie Griffith character, Tess, as she begins her metamorphosis from admin to executive, tells her best friend and fellow admin about a networking function she'll be attending that night for upper managers. Looking over outfits, she holds up a shimmering black dress, calling it "simple and elegant."

"But it needs some bows or somethin'," her friend says, snapping the gum in her mouth.

But Tess explains that she needs a dress like that because she wants to be "interacting with people not as a secretary but as a—"

Her friend cuts her off. "As a total impostor," she says, matter-of-factly.

Tess, a little stunned, stops for a moment, suddenly aware that her admin friend does not understand.

The sad reality of the career lives of many admins is that such inner barriers hold them back all the time. While other professionals take for granted that the level they're currently operating on only marks a staging area for their leap up to the next plateau, many admins tell themselves, without questioning their assumption, that they've reached their limit.

Sales professionals, for example, know that if they work hard they may move up to sales manager, district sales manager, and perhaps VP of sales. Engineers assume the opportunity to rise to senior engineer status, or to some specialized area of expertise, or to project management. Another option might be to break off from employee status altogether and make lots more money as an independent consultant.

But where can the poor admin go? Possibly to a higher level of admin, say as executive admin to the CEO or to some other top officer in the company, but other than that the job stays pretty much the same. You're still just an aide, after all, an administrative support, a gopher, a sentry at the gate. As Carol McDonough said, you're a "nanny for big people."

Though this assumption ain't necessarily the way it has to be, especially in today's changing workplace, a lot of admins presume that it is. The admin who thinks this way then gives up and sinks into the illusion that she's trapped.

Of course, the admin who does feel this way might object. She might tell us: "It's not just the admin, you know. It's also the way admins are treated. There's not a lot we can do about that." And we'd agree with this statement up to a point. Up to the last one, to be exact.

You, as an admin, do have many external forces working against you, as we mentioned in Chapter 1. We realize it's not all you. But other admins have faced the same conditions you do, and yet they've effected big changes in their lives. If they can do it, so can you.

Fighting Your External Forces

In order to prevent these dread external forces from holding you down, we'll need to examine them. As we do this we'll also note a thing or two that you can do about them. Throughout this book you'll encounter many ideas for battling external forces. Some you'll find in the dossiers of real-life ex-admins.

Let's take a look at a few external forces now:

Subtle Signals in the Air

Just as Tess gets the message that trying to be other than an admin amounts to false pretenses, you too may hear or sense similar messages. You'll often catch these signals from bosses, higher-ups, customers, or colleagues. You may even get them from fellow admins, friends, or family.

Remember Bobbi from Chapter 1, who found herself frustrated by her unambitious admin friends?

"All they talk about is men, parties, and outfits," she told us. "I'd like to move up in this company and do something else, like work in marketing or sales, but I don't know how. None of my friends or work colleagues have any ambition."

Recall our advice? We told Bobbi to insist on talking about what she wanted to talk about, and if that didn't work to get some new friends. The first rule, then, is to refuse to let external forces set your agenda for you. In *Working Girl*, Tess has plenty of subtle signals going against her, not only the self-trapping admonitions of her best friend but also the patronizing comments and treacherous actions of her conniving boss, Kathryn (played by Sigourney Weaver; a *woman* boss, no less, who cannot be trusted—ouch!).

But she pushes her way through anyway, setting up her own plan of action and carrying it out methodically. Given the requirements of Hollywood, of course, her plan has to go awry, explode, and involve Harrison Ford. Still, she comes through it all with a very happy ending. But the moral of the story is that it is *possible* for an admin with sufficient spunk to dramatically change her life!

Not-So-Subtle Signals in the Air

Do you work for a company that sets strict criteria for its new hires and transfers? Maybe you're employed by a large bank, for example, that refuses to consider anyone without at least an M.B.A. for any non–admin position, or by an academic institution that hires only professionals with a Ph.D.?

Maybe you work for a company with a clear and obvious "admin track." Once you're on it, you'll be considered for a higher-level admin position, but there's no chance of anything more. Personnel discourages you, your boss discourages you, managers in other departments don't want to risk "stealing away someone else's girl." Direct official barriers to your advancement make it all feel so hopeless.

Throughout this book we'll touch on many ideas for breaking through such barriers. But for the moment, let us leave you with two.

1. Why not go back to school for that bachelor's degree or M.B.A.? Why not *you* with a Ph.D.? Well, why not? As you listen to yourself protest and dredge up excuses, think of this: People, admins and otherwise, do it all the time.
2. Just because a thing has never been done before doesn't mean it can't be. People who blaze new trails are called "pioneers." You could be one too.

Say your company has never moved an admin into a new career area to your, or anyone else's, knowledge. Why couldn't you be the first? You'd obviously have to devise a creative strategy and work real hard at lobbying the right people. You'd have to prepare yourself for a different kind of job interview than what you've been used to, but so what?

Think of yourself as Danielle Boone, Kristina Columbus, or . . . Amelia Earhart!

Subservient Expectations and Demands

Run out right now and rent a movie you've probably already seen once or twice in your life, *Nine to Five.* Go ahead, just put down this book, grab your coat (in Florida, San Diego, and Maui, ignore this step), and get thee to the nearest video store. It's OK. We'll amuse ourselves while you're gone. Just run out and rent a tape of *Nine to Five.* Then come back home and watch it. After the credits, pick up this book again and we'll resume.
[*Pause for viewing of* Nine to Five]

How was that? Wasn't it fun to see that again? Didn't you just love the way the Jane, Dolly, and Lily characters put it to their boss, played by Dabney Coleman? Wouldn't you love to do the same thing to *your* boss, or to one you've had in the past? Wouldn't you just love it?

You surely would if you ever had one who acted in the same repulsive, tyrannical manner that Coleman's character did. For a character like Lily Tomlin's, for example, to keep her talents suppressed beneath the collective male thumbs of the good old boys who owned and ran this company is the height of folly, not only for Lily but for the company as well. Yet openly demanding subservient roles from admins and fostering a "guys" atmosphere is, in fact, the way many companies are set up.

How to fight such an atmosphere in real life? Unlike the Tomlin character's futile attempts to talk to her boss about fetching his coffee as "not being in my job description," your efforts may prove more successful. Simply talking it out may be all you need to do. These days, many male bosses have been forced to rethink previously entrenched attitudes about women's roles in society and will be open to your comments. Others will simply modify their behavior to keep you happy. These bosses do respect you and your work, and they sincerely want you to feel like a valued part of the team.

We'll add here that what we're suggesting by "talk to your boss" is simply that—talk. You don't need to confront, accuse, or throw a fit. That will only confirm the "emotional female" image in the minds of men who don't want to understand (and even many of those who do) and will make things worse. So try talking things out first if you haven't already. Until you do, you can't adequately assess whether or not this simple action step will advance you toward more-respectful relationships.

A second way to reduce subservient expectations is to keep a careful watch on yourself. How do you personally contribute to images of you as the willing office servant-girl? Do people expect you to play this role because you invite them to?

Ethel Cook, a consultant who specializes in "office improvement" issues, and a former admin many times over, rails against admins who volunteer to do domestic chores. "Never offer to hang streamers, take up collections, or serve coffee," she fumes. "Especially never volunteer to bake *anything*! Let others do these things while you take on the task of emceeing an event or organizing the speaker schedule, doing the accounting or some other 'business' task." If you just get involved in stereotypical "helper" roles, Cook insists, especially traditional wife-and-mother tasks, you'll only settle yourself deeper into the pink-collar trap.

As Marg Balcom, now a change management consultant with Millenia Consulting in Natick, Massachusetts (and a former admin herself), puts it, "Support is not subordinate." The former assistant vice president of training at TJ Maxx, Balcom once had bumper stickers printed with these very words and distributed the stickers to support professionals in her recruiting department. "It's all in the way you look at things," she says.

Ethel Cook adds, "If you don't want to be subservient, don't act that way."

Bosses Who Won't Mentor

Everyone works overtime in today's business world. There's always so much to do that if you're not literally pulling down more than forty hours, you're nonetheless likely to be overtaxed mentally, physically, and emotionally in some other way. If you must survive a major layoff, downsizing, or restructuring, you'll undoubtedly end up with more to do than you ever had before. For admins, this development represents both good news and bad news.

The good news is that an admin will possibly find more opportunities to get involved with major projects and important decisions than might ever have been allowed before the cutbacks. With managers and project teams suddenly needing all the extra help and resources they can get, they may start relying on you to do a lot more than type and answer the phone. That means the chance to learn, grow, spend time in other departments, get to know higher-level professionals on an equal basis, and generally build a reputation as a valued player who can be called in to help in a variety of ways.

The downside of such a new order in the work world, however, might be that your manager or supervisor could become so busy and distracted that he'll have less incentive than ever to spend time "developing" his staff. That will especially mean you, the admin, at once his right arm and the bottom of the department totem pole.

He'll also be relying on you more than ever to pull your heaviest admin load. In his harried new frame of mind, the last thing he'll feel he needs is for his sensational, lifesaving admin to be even thinking about leaving. Thus the "Paradox of the Super Admin": The better you are at your work, the more likely you'll get entrenched there. Your good works make it harder and harder for you to get out. You feel like you're digging your own grave.

What to do, what to do? Paul Falcone, a human resources expert and author of *The Complete Job-Finding Guide for Secretaries and Administrative Support Staff,* suggests that the answer may lie in making a mentor out of your boss. Only with your boss's support, Falcone feels, will the chances be good for you to make a move within your present company.

But start your boss off slowly, considering his present stressed-out frame of mind. You might test the waters, Falcone says, by asking him to sign off on an outside training program, preferably on something that could extend your chances for advancement (say, a communications workshop or public speaking or accounting).

"See how your boss reacts," Falcone suggests. Since these programs are frequently quite inexpensive, you'll know that "if this seems too formidable a favor to ask, you've got your answer. It'll be time to look elsewhere." But if your boss does go for it, then you'll have begun to move him into a new frame of mind that will help you get what you want.

A more on-site idea is to volunteer for a special assignment, perhaps one that your boss needs to execute but either doesn't want to or doesn't have time for. Once you get the go-ahead, especially if your boss is willing to supervise you, you'll be home free. You'll both relieve your boss's stress and teach yourself a new set of skills. Any good manager will quickly see what a boon you're becoming. You'll have even saved him the trouble of doing the delegating!

Suppose you know, for example, that your boss needs to execute a cost-accounting project for one of your department's subdivisions. You know too that your boss hasn't exactly been looking forward to this project. Also, despite repeated (and valiant) attempts to find the time, he just hasn't been able to.

One day you walk in all bright and cheery-eyed and lay an action plan on his desk. Handing over an eye-catching, carefully detailed agenda, replete with timelines and clear objectives, you announce, "Here's how I'm suggesting we implement the cost-accounting review for Triple-X Division. I know it's been an impossible project for you to get to, so I'd like to help. If you'll just guide me and answer any questions I might have, I'll do all the calculating, computer inputs, and spreadsheet reviews. You keep checking on me from time to time and by the middle of next quarter, we'll have everything completed."

Wowee zowee! This has got to be sweet, sweet music to your frazzled boss's ears. By virtue of *your* initiative, this vexatious task that just wouldn't go away is finally going to get done. Your suggestions will have expanded your job description *and* created a mentor for you in one fell swoop.

Structure of the Company and/or the Job

Sometimes the very structure of the job or the way a company may be set up can keep you stuck. In a larger company, for example, functions may be so tightly organized that no one is allowed sufficient slack to transfer to a new department or to learn something new. Hiring is always done through search firms whose mandate is to find someone on the outside. That means middle managers, technical personnel, financial professionals—you name it! Even those in upper management feel trapped by the system. No one on any level ever gets the chance to make a move.

Smaller firms too, particularly the smallest ones, may be similarly inflexible. Though as a general rule small firms offer environments that require everyone to pitch in and help with everything, sometimes organizations with extremely specific job functions drive the work atmosphere the other way.

Judy Tyler, now a sales executive with *Premier Bride* magazine, recalls an eye-opening experience at a company she once worked for as an admin.

After many months of doing not much more than what she had been hired to do—mainly to type legal agreements—she expressed her frustration to her boss, the attorney who had hired her, about the lack of intellectual challenge in her duties. The job, she confided, was driving her nuts.

"I need some stimulation," she said. "I need to do something that requires me to think."

Her boss's answer, however, minced no words. "I told you, Judy, during your interview that this job didn't offer much responsibility. I didn't hire you to think. I hired you to type. That's all the job is."

"His blunt response was very motivating," Judy recalls now, laughing. "It motivated me to get the heck out of there! I immediately began taking steps to find a new job."

Inner Barriers

Now let's examine more deeply those "inner barriers" we spoke of earlier, specifically those that block admins from moving ahead in their careers. As much as we might like to foist all the blame for our lot on external forces, most of the responsibility for lingering in an unsatisfactory job will usually rest on our own two shoulders. We are only human, after all, suffering to one degree or another a myriad of neuroses, self-doubts, and lapses in self-esteem. Some of these afflictions are common to admins, a product of the external forces in their environments as well as symptomatic of the personality type that gets attracted to, and perpetuated by, this work.

Hear for yourself the observations of a lineup of admins, ex-admins and "guest experts" who have either experienced these inner barriers at work or studied them in others. See how many "self-trapping mechanisms" you've noticed in yourself:

Angela Maffeo, former admin for CPA and legal firms, now a career and lifestyles counselor: "A lot of admins fall into unfortunate codependent relationships with their bosses or supervisors. They ought to see these work relationships as partnerships, but instead codependency wins out. They have difficulty setting boundaries and end up doing too much for others, giving away too much of themselves. Many, many admins are not even conscious of it."

Anne Marie Dangler, executive secretary: "You deal with a lot of egos in this job and that feeds on your own sense of self-esteem. You feel low on the totem pole, not valued. In light of this, a lot of admins never learn to speak up for themselves. They never learn to be assertive, though it's a necessity. Staying quiet all the time, not speaking up, keeps them in the same place and they never get ahead."

Carol McDonough, executive admin: "Many admins aren't confident in themselves. They're too nice to everybody. They don't learn to deflect bullets, so they get shot down a lot. And they stay down."

Ethel Cook, veteran admin, now professional organizer, trainer, consultant, and motivational speaker: "Many admins don't see themselves as part of the management team or even as professionals. I moved myself ahead by forcing myself to grow and thus developing my self-esteem. Too many admins don't work hard enough at that."

Judy Tyler, former admin, now a sales executive with *Premier Bride* magazine: "It's the 'female role' that keeps admins stuck—putting someone else's needs before your own. That's tough to break out of because you're constantly focusing on someone else's needs."

Cary Schwartz, former office temp, now a high school math teacher: "There's a sense a lot of admins have of 'Why bother?' They'll settle into comfortable routines and get complacent. You get a sense that they didn't really want to do any more than they're doing now. To do more would invite expectation and potential failure."

Mary Miller, ex–executive admin, now marketing manager at a major university: "Being female is the first thing on the list. I grew up with the subtle message that I didn't have a brain, I didn't know enough. That breeds fear of success, as well as a more subtle fear of failure. When I think about the times I was successful at things while growing up, I recall people being jealous of me. Not many rejoiced with me."

Paul Falcone, author of *The Complete Job-Finding Guide for Secretaries and Administrative Support Staff:* "I heard an employment trainer talking once about the two basic mentalities operating in the work world today. He called them 'factory' and 'entrepreneurial' mentalities.

"Factory thinkers compose a major segment of our 'entitlement culture.' They're always looking for safe jobs, lifelong jobs, secure salaries. Entrepreneurial mentalities, instead, take on risk. There's a global perspective there, a willingness to see how they might fit into the overall organization. They'll routinely reach beyond their job descriptions and offer up a higher value.

"Unfortunately, I've found many admins only want to approach their jobs with the factory mentality. They shy away from entrepreneurial thinking. They just don't choose to take enough risks."

Judy Wagner, ex-admin, now a counseling assistant with an EAP provider: "Sometimes, of course, it's a lifestyle choice. You can walk away from admin work at the end of the day and stop working for a while. You might simply be happy doing what you're doing, and you're not interested in climbing the corporate ladder. In that way, lack of a career development plan holds you back, as does the very lack of a desire for a career. Though if it's a lifestyle freely chosen, there's nothing wrong with it."

Nancy Cassesso, former secretary, now a sales professional with a manufacturers' rep: "I held myself back for a number of years because I simply didn't think I could do the job that I do now. I'd been offered the chance before, but I turned it down. I just didn't have enough confidence in my abilities."

Rusty Stieff, former admin, now vice president in the nonprofit lending group at a major commercial bank: "Often it's the squeaky wheel thing—if you don't make any noise, nobody notices you. A lot of admins fail to make it clear to others that they even want to move up."

Susan Schenkel, Ph.D., author of *Giving Away Success: Why Women Get Stuck and What to Do About It:* "But when left to projects of our own initiative, [women] flounder. Typically we describe ourselves as people who don't follow through or who drop out. Our lives are full of unfinished projects: uncompleted college degrees, course work, resumés, painting, and books.

"Learning how to be helpless makes women vulnerable to interpreting any serious difficulty as evidence of inevitable failure. Pulling out appears to be the most reasonable course of action. After all, why beat a dead horse?"

Kind of makes your head spin, doesn't it? There's a lot of work to do, it seems, a lot of change that has to go on inside. Of course, we're not saying that all of the inner barriers mentioned here belong to you. You may be way ahead of the game with some of them. But others may be getting the best of you and, if that is so, it's critical that you know that.

By identifying your inner barriers, you'll contain and corral them, wrestle them into submission, maybe even set them loose to run away from you and hassle someone else. The main point to remember is that *you* are the boss here. You can do anything you want with your inner barriers—ship them off to a different department, make them sit in a corner without any lunch, hand them a pink slip. But what you've got to know first is what they look like.

"Life-Point Analysis"

To identify your inner barriers, you place them within the context of your whole life. Your barriers typically surround themselves with your fears and anxieties about who you are, what you're capable of, what the world expects from you. They want to help you, they really do, and you should pay attention to what they're trying to say. But you should never let them hold the reins.

In the frame on the next page, draw a picture of yourself. Yes, you heard us right: *Draw* a picture of yourself. In fact, if you rummage about your house or office for some crayons or markers, you may end up having a lot of fun with this! C'mon, let's head back to childhood, when we never much cared about self-

Portrait of ME!

esteem, insecurity, or fear of success or failure. We were having too much fun!

Don't read further until you've finished your self-portrait.

Now that you've completed your self-portrait, go back and insert positive and negative "life points" that populate your life. Include talents, skills, dreams, and proud achievements as well as fears, anxieties, worries, and bad habits. Insert your positive and negative "life points" by drawing them all around your self-portrait. Do not use any numbers, letters, or words. (That's correct. You read us right again: no numbers, words, or letters—just drawings.)

Use your natural creativity and let yourself have some fun. When you have finished, resume reading.

Now, let's evaluate what you've done. Contemplate these questions:

1. *What happened when we asked you to tackle this assignment?* Did you enthusiastically grab a box of markers or crayons and excitedly whip together your self-portrait? If so, that one step—picking up crayons or markers—something you did even before the official exercise began, showed a willingness in you to do whatever it takes to advance your career and personal growth. You trusted that trying something different might advance you a little bit further. You took a chance. Good show!

2. *What did you fret a bit (or a lot!) about drawing a picture of yourself?* Did you think at once, "Me, draw? I could never do that—I'd be laughed out of my house and home!" If you felt even a tinge of this but went ahead anyway, you too showed the willingness to brave your fears. You took a risk despite an inner barrier that tried to stop you. Double good show!

3. *How'd you do on the next part, adding in your "life points"?* Did you struggle at times to find a way to depict good and bad points without using numbers, letters, or words? If you did, but you fought bravely through anyway, know this: Whatever you put on the page, no matter how it looks, demonstrated your innate ability to be creative. It doesn't matter at all what it looks like, either (tell your cat to stop laughing). You simply devised a

way to communicate something in a new way. That, friend, we call creativity.

4. *On the flip side, did you get down on yourself because you couldn't think of a way to pictorialize every point?* Did you worry you might not have executed this exercise perfectly? If so, please be warned: Perfectionism's an occupational hazard for admins, whose job is to take care of all the details, dotting the boss's *i*'s, crossing his *t*'s. When it comes to you personally, it's a skill that often gets you in trouble.

Let your perfectionism go. You can't move forward if you demand too much of yourself. You'll only stress yourself out and hesitate taking a next step. And you've *got* to take next steps: They're your lifeblood, they're the principal career activities that will spring you from the pink-collar ghetto. Don't feel you need to do everything perfectly. Just do it well.

FROM THE ADMIN FILES

Name of ex-admin: Janet Hartford-Hill

Currently: Antique dealer, Dallas, Texas

Admin skills used today: Time management, social interaction skills

How change was made: "I'd always kept fun items on my desk wherever I worked as an admin. I loved to go antiquing on the weekends: I was always at a swap meet or county fair or dropping in on an antique shop. If I was on vacation, the first thing I'd do was check the local papers and see what antique shows might be in the area. (This drives my husband nuts!)

"One weekend while I was at an auction, I met an old friend I hadn't seen since high school. I asked her what she was doing, and she told me, 'I hunt for things I can sell.'

" 'You can make a living at this?' I asked.

" 'A darn good one,' my friend said.

"I was off and running after that. First I picked her brain for everything she'd ever learned about how to buy and sell old items. Then I got to know some of her friends in the business. Before I knew what I was really doing, I'd given notice to my employer. After twelve years as an admin, I became a professional 'antiquer.' "

Best advice for admins: "Look to your hobbies and personal interests for ideas. Don't take yourself for granted."

3

The Fear-of-Failure Gang

If our inner barriers showed up regularly on the TV program *America's Most Wanted*, the one barrier that most Americans would *really* want to see captured—the kingpin of them all—would be Fear of Failure, also known by its alias, Fear of Success. Like some monstrous gang boss, this barrier towers wickedly over all the others, keeping conditions safe for your other inner barriers to run their numbers on you. Maybe that's why it can be so tough at times to accurately distinguish between Fear of Failure, Fear of Success, and fear of this, that, and everything else. Our failure fears can be just that enormous.

In our work over the years with career-minded professionals, Fear of Failure/Success invariably rears its troublesome head sooner or later. CEO, admin, financial consultant, security guard—it really doesn't matter who you are. Undoubtedly you have struggled with your own version of the fear barrier.

In Jan Halper's book *Quiet Desperation: The Truth About Successful Men*, male CEOs discuss their innermost feelings about their successful climbs to the top. Surprisingly, Halper's results reveal tremendous levels of fear inside these men in relation to the very implications of their career successes.

They worry, for example, about being able to continue their success, about greater responsibilities created by each new success, about what they would do if suddenly, somehow, they lost their job. Despite proving their abilities again and again, these men still had to shore up their confidence every day against their fears of what failure and even success could bring.

So fear of failure/success isn't limited to admins. Instead it's a universal problem, an ingredient we manufacture naturally that gets us into trouble because sometimes we pay the wrong attention to it. We automatically give it the power to dominate us, to tell us what to do. "If I'm afraid," we reason, "I must not be doing the right thing." Yet often we know, deep down, we *are* doing the right thing. What goes on, simply, is that we feel scared, and since we don't enjoy that feeling we try to get rid of it in any way we can. The easiest way (we reason erroneously) is to succumb to its wishes.

Ethel Cook, now an independent consultant, recalls a career experience that illustrates what we mean.

Once, as an admin, Ethel had successfully put together an important conference of her company's major executives. Her boss was so pleased with her work that he wanted to acknowledge her for it in front of all the attendees.

"Ethel, it's only right you get credit for what you've done here. This meeting wouldn't be taking place without you. I'm going to introduce you to everyone, and then I'd like you to say a few words. Just say hello and maybe thank everyone for coming—it doesn't have to be much. I just think you deserve a few moments in the sun."

Ethel freaked out. "I won't do it," she said. "I can't get up there in front of everyone and give a speech. I can't do it. I won't do it."

"No, no, not a speech, Ethel, just a few words. You don't have to say much, just 'Hello, thank you for coming,' then sit down."

Ethel was still terrified. What if her voice gave out? What if people laughed at her? What if she sounded like an idiot? She couldn't do this; she couldn't successfully pull this off, not even for the briefest moment.

"No, I won't do it," she declared vehemently. "And if you make me do it, I'll quit!" Her boss had to give in. She was simply not going to stand up in front of all those people.

Deep within, Ethel knew she was yielding to her fears and losing something in the bargain. Intellectually, she knew she could, in fact, do this, that she might even succeed at it. But fear of failure (in front of an audience, no less) had blinded her from taking a necessary, if scary, first step.

As the years went by, Ethel developed a desire to leave admin work and become an independent consultant. She knew, however, that this work would require her to do lots and lots of public speaking. With her fears still gripping her inside, she began attending Toastmasters', a public-speaking club, and taking every opportunity she could find to get up in front of an audience. She got actively involved with a national seminar company and with the National Speakers Association, and now, years later, she commands "a substantial fee," she says, for giving a talk or seminar. She admits, too, that she still gets nervous before a presentation, but now she doesn't let her anxiety keep her down. Her fear still lives, but it no longer functions as a barrier to her success.

Fear as a Signal to Grow

Obviously, letting our fears run our lives rules out exciting opportunities for career advancement. Ethel might have embarked on her successful career as a consultant and speaker years earlier had she accepted her boss's invitation to just say hello and thank everyone. Of course, all of us can look back on our lives, both professional and personal, and recall similar incidents when our fears held us back from doing something we knew would take us forward.

Yet, when new opportunities arise, we fall into the same trap. It's a frame of mind we too easily fall into. To get out of this frame of mind, we need to substitute a new one. What if we saw failure, for example, as a learning experience? That's after all what it really is, an opportunity to discover how to do something in order to eventually discover how to do it right, and well.

Susan Schenkel, in *Giving Away Success*, puts it like this:

> Since by definition a challenge isn't a sure thing and some failure is inevitable, failure must be viewed as a temporary setback that creates an opportunity to learn. It becomes a cue to try something else, not a signal to withdraw. Sustained effort in the face of setbacks allows one to persist long enough to attain success.

This in turn reinforces a more optimistic attitude toward future failures.

Schenkel should know what she's talking about. She's studied the subject for many years and taught courses on it at major universities. She's also observed the dynamics of failure-as-a-barrier and "sustained effort" as a method of breakthrough in the clients she sees in her psychology practice. We've observed the same dynamics in our career exploration programs.

Sarah, an admin working for a company based in Pittsburgh, told us the following story.

An opportunity to travel to the company's Northwest branch had come up. Although qualified to represent her company on these service missions—she'd handled hundreds of client inquiries and problems over the years and knew the company's products inside and out—Sarah immediately began thinking: "I'm afraid to ask for this assignment because I don't know what my boss, Jim, would say. What if he laughed in my face? He might think I'm not capable of going out to see clients by myself, that I don't know enough, that I'm just a [gulp!] admin! I have no idea what Jim would say."

At first she gave in to the fear. "I won't go ask him. It's better that I don't know what he thinks. Hearing his negative thoughts about me would be devastating. Besides, what if he took a chance on me and I blew it?"

After a few sleepless nights, Sarah decided, "Forget it! What if I do blow it? If I don't even try, how can I ever succeed? How can I ever move to a better job? Besides, if Jim does say no, at least I'll be able to get some sleep again!"

The next day, revving up her courage, she went to Jim's office to ask him about the assignment. At first Jim in fact did hem and haw a bit about her going alone. "You've never done this before," he said. "How do I know you can handle it?"

Braving her own self-doubts, Sarah began to speak and within seconds heard herself telling Jim about her strengths and abilities: "I'm very good with customers on the phone, Jim—you know that—and I solve a lot of their problems on my own, when no one else is in the office. I almost never run to you anymore with a question, do I? I know most of the time exactly where to go for the right answer."

Was her voice wavering too much as she made her case? Was she subtly revealing her deepest anxieties about failing? Sarah didn't know but she pressed on. After listening to all she had to say, Jim pulled out a travel voucher and put Sarah's name on it. "You're right," he said, nodding his head. "You've come a long way since that day you walked in here as a temp. Let's get you on a flight to Seattle and see what you can do."

Rather than let her fears stop her, Sarah realized they were signposts for growth. We fear something because it represents something new, unfamiliar. Our adrenalin gets pumping as we wonder: Can I do this? But we also realize we'll never know unless we try. So we push through our fears, as Sarah did, and ask for, or take, the job.

And that's the key ingredient, experts will tell you, in breaking through fears, doubts, and anxieties and getting on with life. Don't let your Fear of Failure (or of Success) hold back your actions. Fear can make you examine an opportunity to see if it's right for you. It can pique your senses. But your ultimate decision should never be based on Fear of Failure alone. Failure plainly must be experienced now and then if we are to also experience success.

Fear of Success

Regarding Fear of Success, what is it really but just a variation of Fear of Failure? Like those CEOs in the book *Quiet Desperation*, it's only a postponement of the inevitable. It reveals a deep-seated insecurity about one's intrinsic ability. Listen to a few statements from admins who shared their deepest feelings about this subject in our career programs:

Sylvia, who works for a real estate firm in White Plains, New York: "When I succeed at doing a great job at a new project, won't that just postpone failure to a future date? When I succeed, I'm often just lucky, or somebody's giving me a break. People simply haven't seen through me yet. So what's the point of succeeding? They'll just find out I'm incompetent later."

Betsy, employed by a construction company in Provo, Utah: "If I succeed, I might not like what I've succeeded at, and I'll be disappointed. If I get disappointed, there must be something wrong with my ability to make decisions. It'll highlight my poor sense of judgment, which I already feel I have. Why go through all that? Maybe I'd better just stay where I am and quit kidding myself."

Mary-Margaret, working for a small manufacturing firm in Vermont: "I always wonder if I really deserve to succeed even when I do. I'm always thinking, 'This isn't me, this isn't me. You may think I'm a competent person, but I'm not as good as you believe.' It's some strong, strong doubt that's deep inside me. It makes me want to get as far away from my success as I can."

Can you see how Fear of Success seems to feed off Fear of Failure? "If I succeed, it'll either postpone failure or risk people finding out I didn't deserve to succeed in the first place," we think. "Or it'll show off my other failings, like poor judgment." Gee whiz, you can't win for losing, can you?

Fear Breakers

Enough talk! Let's get down to putting some of our fears to rest. Or at least to identifying what we can do about them so they don't keep holding us back.

On the worksheet on the next page, list your career fears. You may list Fear of Failure, Fear of Success, or any other fears that come to mind. If we want to contain or eradicate our fears, we've first got to get them clearly out in the open.

After you've listed all your fears, move to the right-hand column and list an idea for braving each fear. Don't worry about how confident you are about your idea working (that's only another example of your fear!). Just jot it down. As time goes by, you'll have the chance to try out your ideas and see which work and which don't. If an idea doesn't work, of course, you've still accomplished something: You'll have risked, and experienced, failure, but you won't have let it hold you back!

Fear	*Idea for Braving This Fear*
1. _____	_____
	_____
	_____.
2. _____	_____
	_____
	_____.
3. _____	_____
	_____
	_____.
4. _____	_____
	_____
	_____.
5. _____	_____
	_____
	_____.

Most experts who study human fears, and admins who have successfully prevented their fears from holding them back, tend to agree on one remedy: action! No matter how difficult, frightening, worrisome the fear, the best way to eradicate it or gain control over it is to do something about it. In her excellent book *Feel the Fear and Do It Anyway*, Susan Jeffers offers a central message you might give yourself while initiating such actions: "Whatever comes as a result of facing my fears, I can handle it."

And she's right, you know. Our most basic fear is that we won't be able to handle whatever unknown or unpredictable result comes our way because of our actions. We don't believe we're capable of dealing with the ramifications of facing our fears on our own. Maybe our fear or anxiety is really an ancient primeval instinct alerting us to keep our senses clear, our heads up, and all our wits about us. "Do your best, your absolute best, with everything working at full capacity," might be another way of saying it.

But whatever you do, don't hang back and do nothing. You really can handle it.

Sarah, for example, "handled" the momentary ambivalence expressed by her boss, Jim, by refusing to let it affect her. She felt her gravest fears rising anew as he wondered aloud about her abilities. But she kept to her plan, kept talking. She didn't stop, run, hide, or back down. She continued acting.

Ethel Cook, later in her career, finally stood up at a podium for the first time and risked all the laughter, ridicule, disapproval she'd feared for so many years. But it didn't materialize, and that only made her a little stronger and more confident to stand up at a podium a second time, then a third, and a fourth, and again and again. Over time, she became a seasoned professional speaker, still with fears, but in control of them.

The Helper Mentality

A charter member of the Fear of Failure Gang, the nefarious Helper Mentality makes its appearance throughout the work world in many guises, all donned primarily by women. Mostly female nurses, for example, are the helpers of mostly male doctors (and mostly female nurses' aides help the nurses!). Mostly female faculty assistants help out mostly male professors in academia. Mostly female human resources professionals help out mostly male managers in business.

Other professional helpers, again mostly women, include therapists, social workers, counselors, customer service staff, and teachers and trainers. Anything primarily viewed as a "helping" role, it seems, will tend to draw most of its practitioners from the ranks of women.

Janice LaRouche, author (with Regina Ryan) of *Janice La-Rouche's Strategies for Women at Work*, labels this phenomenon "The Helpmate Block." In her comprehensive exploration of inner barriers that directly affect professional women, LaRouche explains:

Playing the traditional helpmate is a hard habit to break. Not only is it ingrained in us as the truly feminine way to be, but it is also part of a deal: I help you become successful, and you take the ultimate responsibility for my welfare.

Many women, instead of focusing on what they can get out of the workplace, typically spend much of their energy looking for opportunities to give. Yet seeing themselves in this way—as givers, not takers; as helpers, not leaders—stops women from figuring out the real needs of a situation and how best to respond. It stops them from taking initiative and accepting responsibility. And it prevents them from doing what's best for themselves and for their own careers.

Only by giving up this support role, LaRouche insists, can women helpers truly learn to support themselves. That's because the mere act of letting go of the compulsion to support others (to the exclusion of one's own needs) puts an end to a concurrent overreliance on others for support. She suggests that when we stop caring "too much" about others and expecting others to care "too much" about us, we begin filling up our caring gap by focusing attention and support on ourselves.

Admins, whether women or men, should heed LaRouche's advice. It's an occupational hazard, like perfectionism: You spend every minute of your workday toiling to assist someone else (or a crew of someone elses), so there's precious little time or energy left over to think about yourself. In some ways, of course, there's nothing new about this.

Back in what we might call the Age of Loyalty, when job security was in flower, workers knew that by doing their jobs the best they knew how they would be rewarded, promoted, or, at the very least, kept working by their employers. Little time or attention need be accorded to extracurricular career development. You took care of someone else (your boss), he took care of you. That simple.

Sometime during the 1980s, however, the music died and the Age of Loyalty came to an end. Now no one can merely do her job and take for granted it'll still be there even a week from now. We've all got to have a plan. We've all got to help ourselves.

Self-Support Mind Map

One way to help you speed this process along might be through a Self-Support Mind Map.

Have you ever heard of a mind map? It's a creativity technique for exploring an issue by opening it up to the artistic corners of your brain. It's a nonlinear, daydreamish approach that takes the perspective of problems-as-discovery. It also lets you examine an issue over time by allowing for ongoing inputs and ideas.

You can construct your own Self-Support Mind Map by scrawling the words *How I Support Me* in the center of a sheet of poster paper (or two or more 8^1/$_2$ by 11 sheets of paper taped together), as shown in Figure 3-1. Using markers or crayons, map out—via tentacles or wavy lines—key characteristics, vexing problems, goals, potential solutions, next steps, and supportive resources.

At the end of each line or tentacle, you might write such categories as "Career desires," "Personal life," "Educational interests," "Actions I must take," "People who can help *me*," "Resources I can call on," and so on. Then you draw pictures along each line and/or shoot off secondary lines/tentacles from the main lines to denote subpoints and side issues.

For example, subpoints of "Educational interests" might include "Finishing my degree," "Taking relevant workshops," "Reading more books." You'll then make notes to yourself around these points, such as "Call colleges for course catalogs," "Go to library and scan computer section," or "Check with adult-ed center for relevant workshops." Some of these elements, or subpoints, might connect naturally with each other (say, "Reading more books" with "Career desires"). If so, run a dotted line between the two and show the connection.

To make the whole thing truly colorful and fun, paste in magazine excerpts, photos, quotes, and cartoons. Attach relevant objects if they'll fit: a ribbon, a button, a fortune from a fortune cookie. In short, make your mind map a collage of your

Figure 3-1. Sample "How I Support Me" Mind Map

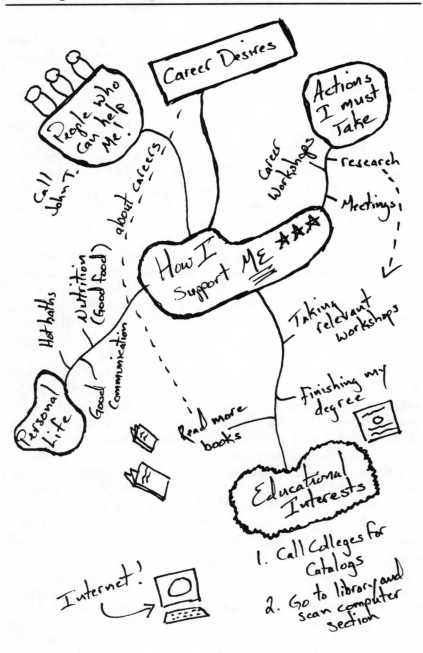

thinking and imagination. Let it grow and grow until you have the fullest, most vibrant understanding of how to actively support yourself as you successfully advance your career.

To keep your exploration of this issue alive, take a look at your mind map every day and keep adding to it or changing it. Tape it on your bedroom or office wall, where you can easily see it. As time goes on, your Self-Support Mind Map will evolve organically, as will your ideas and resolve about achieving your goals.

Achievement Deficiency

What are you proud of? What accomplishments in your life do you recall enthusiastically? Can you immediately come up with two or three good ones? How about twenty or thirty good ones? Or does your mind instead go blank when we ask such questions? If it does, you're undoubtedly a victim of another certified member of the Fear of Failure Gang: Achievement Deficiency.

Admins display a notorious, almost gleeful, capacity to discount their abilities and achievements. They often assume that anything they've done can be chalked up to luck, or to someone else's help (the Helper Mentality!), or that a task they've done or talent they have is really nothing very special. In *Giving Away Success*, Susan Schenkel cites this all too common inner barrier as particularly ingrained in women.

"There are many ways we discount ourselves," she writes, explaining that "when women are successful, it must be explained in some other way." Schenkel calls this the "feminine discounting habit," depriving women of ongoing positive feedback. Missing out on such feedback, she says, locks out information needed to make "optimistic predictions." This prevents confidence-building and the upgrading of "unrealistically low expectations."

She concludes that, to the extent women attribute success to luck, easy tasks, or other people's efforts, "we tell ourselves that we aren't in control of our environment." Hence, Achievement Deficiency, the idea that you've never really done anything special in your life and probably never will. Achievement Deficiency declares, "I'm just not that good, special, or powerful."

Young girls in particular have been taught to heed this sign. While boys may be encouraged to scale a wall, girls will be advised to not even try it. They might get hurt, fail, or—God forbid—get dirty!!

One of us (Ken) recalls distinctly a curriculum track in his high school during the 1960s called "the commercial course." Other school systems back then called this "the business course" or even "the secretarial program." A boy, as Ken recalls, rarely enrolled in that curriculum—or, if he did, everyone wondered about him. Any male who truly dreamed of getting involved in the business world naturally took classes in "the college curriculum" and went on to higher education. Commercial, business, and secretarial programs were for girls only.

Small wonder then that legions of admins graduate from their educational experiences each year believing they can contribute little more than merely helping out their more highly achieving male bosses. Even those who understand the counterproductivity of such thinking still "diss" themselves by playing down their accomplishments. Somewhere along the way they learned it just wasn't feminine. Thus, much of the dissing of admins gets reinforced by their own words and actions.

Achievement Roll Call

One way to get this Fear of Failure Gang member off your back is to get more in touch with the reality of your life achievements—to think about them, write them down, read them, certify that they're true. It's too easy to forget that you really did these things, *you really did.*

So let's line a few up for inspection and pay them some heed. On the accompanying worksheet, list at least eight professional achievements. If you can think of more, grab another sheet of paper and list them too.

Beside each achievement, note the reasons you feel good about what you achieved. When you have finished making this list, read on.

Achievements	**Why You're Proud**
1. _____	_____
2. _____	_____
3. _____	_____
4. _____	_____
5. _____	_____
6. _____	_____
7. _____	_____
8. _____	_____

How did you do? Did you complete the list? If you didn't, go back and complete it now. Yes, yes, you have indeed achieved at least a few great things over the course of your career. Now go back and think harder.

Looking at Your List

Now how did you do? We bet you surprised yourself! Did you come up with more achievements than you thought you would before you started? What reasons did you come up with for each achievement? What do your reasons say about you, about the kind of person you are, about your capabilities?

Your completed list will paint a picture of a very powerful human being. It shows your capacity for accomplishing most anything you set your mind to. Can you remember how you felt before you set your sights on these eventual achievements? Maybe you were scared, anxious, self-doubting. But you pushed through these inner barriers anyway; you faced down your fears and made it through.

Well, guess what? You can do that again.

Most people (not just admins) find this assignment daunting at first. If you didn't, if you just enjoyed it and mustered your enthusiasm for it and completed it quickly, then score a big fat A-plus for yourself! If you struggled with the list, but you pushed yourself through to completing it anyway, you get an A-plus too!

If you didn't complete the list, though, it's time for you to do so. Look, we know you can do this and so do you. Just go back there, young lady, and finish up; it's all going to be fine. We'll leave your A-plus waiting for you here on the edge of your desk. Pick it up when you're done with your list.

Recording your achievements and taking note of the personal abilities you employ to make things happen can help you keep your personal power in view. Whenever you find yourself doubting your talent and potential, just whip out this list and take a look at it. By then, you'll undoubtedly have a new achievement or two to add to it.

By regularly renewing your understanding about how capable you are, you'll also renew and reinvigorate your confidence in attaining your career (and life) dreams.

The Overwhelm Factor

How do you like the title of this section? Doesn't *The Overwhelm Factor* sound like a movie starring Michael Caine and Brenda Vaccaro? Michael Caine's a British agent dashing through the busy, rainy streets of London, pulling Brenda along with him as she tries to hold on to her broad-brimmed hat. Big Ben is tolling in the background, but they've got to get to Scotland Yard before the bomb goes off in Buckingham Palace. Get there too late, and it's curtains for the Queen, England, and the Empire. . . . *The Overwhelm Factor*, a Miramax/United Artists release, coming this Christmas to a video store near you.

Well—surprise!—the Overwhelm Factor actually refers to yet another member of the Fear of Failure Gang, another inner barrier common to admins. And—double surprise!—we have a *real* motion picture in mind that will help describe the Overwhelm Factor: the film *What About Bob?*, popular a few years back.

In this "screwball American comedy," as the ads like to say, Richard Dreyfuss plays a noted psychiatrist who has written a best-selling book called *Baby Steps*. He hopes the message of his book will help daffy, neurotic Bill Murray get his life together—so that he will leave Dreyfuss and his family, vacationing at a lake resort, alone! But need we add that dealing with a Bill Murray character, it doesn't work? That's all we're going to say about the movie's plot.

Interestingly, back here in real life, we find the message of Dreyfuss's *Baby Steps* "book" very instructive. We think the movie's writers really had something there.

Feeling a bit overwhelmed, anyone? Having trouble with what life seems to have handed you? You say you've seen the Big Picture but you're not sure you can handle it?

Your solution is simple: Take a few baby steps!

Many admins stop themselves in their tracks whenever an obstacle in their career path looms too large. Though admins will think nothing of taking on large-scale, derring-do projects for their bosses, staying late until all hours, tunneling through mountains of paperwork, typing, spell-checking, filing until the cows come home, they'll less frequently take on the same challenges for just themselves. That's when all the other fears kick in at the same time. Fear of Failure, Fear of Success, the Helper Mentality, Achievement Deficiency—they all show up.

So take baby steps. One step forward, that's it; stretch one foot out in front of you, that's right. Now put it down again. Goooood! You're getting the idea.

Now the other foot. I know this feels shaky but, ahhh, that's it, get it out there. Good again. By George, I think she's got it! You're *two* steps forward now—would you take a look at that! You're on your way!

When faced with a seemingly overwhelming project, break it down into stages, steps, or tiny pieces. What may seem like one heck of an impossible task can actually get accomplished with a considerably lighter load of stress. You might not even know for sure where you're really going, what the end of the road you're on will look like. But one thing you probably do know: You can't stay where you are and make everything change.

So remember the old Chinese adage: "A journey of a thousand miles must begin with a single step." Remember that each new step brings you closer. Even baby steps.

MY LIFE AS A TEMP—FORMER MALE ADMIN CARY SCHWARTZ

Now a high school math teacher, Cary Schwartz worked for Kelly Services as a temp early in his career. He quickly moved into the credit industry and later, after going back to school for a master's degree, into high school teaching. He reflects here on differences between men and women he observed during his temping days and differences he sees today in his classes.

"I didn't type and I was male, so I guess that pegged me. I didn't get many assignments in highly visible places, like reception lobbies or as someone's personal secretary. They seemed to put me in a lot of basements instead.

"I remember much of my temping days as so totally mindless. One job I had, I'd be looking up customer information in these big giant log books, hundreds and hundreds of pages. There weren't any computers in this company yet (it was about 1987), so my job was to physically look up a customer's name and verify that the info was correct. I sat with another temp all day long, and we both thought the job was hysterical. We seemed to be laughing all day long.

"Another time I was stationed in a huge room with some kind of weird gigantic circular filing unit that kept swinging around in circles, in and out of the wall. People would come in and hand me a file and bark at me. 'File this,' they'd say, then walk out. That was the whole job.

"Then there was a job in which they put me in a room in the basement of this bank, and to tell you the truth I can't remember now what they wanted me to do down there. All I can remember is that if I didn't have a radio on down there, I went nuts.

"Of the other temps I'd meet, I didn't sense a lot of ultimate goals in their lives. I was usually the only male and, looking back on it, now that I've been a high school teacher, I think that may have had a lot to do with male-female conditioning. For example, I notice that the boys in my classes are always louder than the girls, and that intimidates many of the girls. The girls' work itself is generally of higher quality but their participation suffers, their willingness to take a chance, to risk failure in front of others. And even with the awareness I have of trying not to favor boys over girls, I still see girls getting edged out by the boys and holding back.

"Maybe that's what was going on back in those temp jobs. I always knew temping would not be permanent for me. I never saw it as anything more than a fun phase as I moved on to something else.

"But for a lot of the women who did it, I think they had already given up. It sometimes seemed to be a sense of 'why bother?' The fewer risks you took, the fewer mistakes you could make. Why spoil a good thing? These jobs were 'easy' and 'comfortable.' Controlled, predictable, secure. At least they seemed that way.

"So could school have done it to them, then the workplace? Don't take any chances, don't compete with the boys, don't even try? Especially in the workplace where it was only fun to me because it seemed so absurd. I know now that if you can inject some fun into a learning atmosphere and take away the consequences of being wrong ('You're fired!' or 'You failed!'), then people will be willing to try anything, to experiment, to learn."

FROM THE ADMIN FILES

Name of ex-admin: Nancy Cassesso

Currently: Sales associate for office- and school-supply company, maintaining accounts with established customers and marketing new products

Admin skills used today: "If customers called and needed something, as an admin I would help them out. I do essentially the same thing now, only I do it out of the office as well as inside. Admin work helped me understand how to handle paperwork efficiently, how to prepare for a meeting, and how to respond quickly."

How change was made: "I held myself back for a long time. This job was actually offered to me a few years ago, when I was working for the company as an admin, but I turned it down. I didn't think I could handle it. Things changed when I started taking more risks in my life, both professional and personal, and believing in myself. Now when people say, 'I'm just a secretary' or 'I'm only an admin,' I get annoyed.''

Best advice for admins: ''Explore any and all possibilities that intrigue you. You'll never know what you can do until you try.''

4

What's Unique About *You?*

Imagine you are holding a mega-lottery ticket in your hand. Yes, we understand: You'd never ever buy a lottery ticket; that's not your style. We know that. You think lotteries are such a long shot, no one ever really wins them—at least no one you've ever met. Certainly *you* could never win.

Even so, let's suppose, on a whim, in a rare fit of insanity, you bought a ticket earlier today for this week's upcoming, stupendous $56 million jackpot. The devil made you do it.

Now it's time for *Lottery Live!* on TV. Again, we know you'd never be caught dead watching this five-minute on-air homage to legalized gambling, but for some reason tonight you do. (El Diablo again!) Actually, you hadn't planned to but you were flipping channels and suddenly—babagazinga!—there's the snazzy opening jingle and here's that ticket you purchased earlier that day, right there on your coffee table. "Oh, what the heck," you think. "I bought the darned thing, didn't I? Why not see what comes up?"

A moment later, the lottery machine's Ping-Pong balls go zipping about in their cages, then drop one by one into preset slots. The number 3 comes down first, then 4, then 3 again. You glance somewhat bemusedly at your ticket. You have 3 and 4 too, you notice. Ha-ha. Funny. Then, a little startled, you notice that your third number, like that on the screen, is also 3.

Despite your better judgment, your heart begins to beat a little faster. Your second three numbers are 5, 7, and 2. Surely, there's no chance that . . . The next ball on the screen drops. It's 5.

Is your heart beating faster still now? You bet it is. The next ball comes down. "It couldn't possibly be a seven," you say out loud, though there's no one else in the room. What could I be thinking of? The ball slides into place. It's . . . 7!

Holy winner's circle, Batman! If the next number's a 2, you're a millionaire fifty-six times over. Lord above, what're the odds? The last ball drops. "Me, me, me," you cry out loud. Then you start chanting, "2, 2, 2, 2." You're more spiritual tonight than you've ever been in your whole life. "Please, God, please," you pray. You're also like some maniac up on the roof of Caesar's Palace in Las Vegas. "C'mon, 2!" you scream, "2, 2, 2, 2!"

The ball slides into place. Know what? *It's a 2!* People hear you roar all the way to the Fiji Islands. *"I won! I won!"* That lottery ticket in your clammy, shaking hand is worth 56 million dollars. *You're rich!*

Question: Now What Would You Do If You Were Really Rich?

Write down everything you would do in the first twenty minutes of your newfound abundance. Keep yourself right there in the moment, right in front of your TV, in your living room. What exactly do you do next?

1. _____

_____

_____

_____

_____

2. _____

_____

_____

_____

_____

3. _____

_____

_____

_____

_____

4. _____

_____

_____

_____

_____

5. _____

_____

_____

_____

_____

After you've fainted, picked yourself up, called friends, spouse, family, your grocer, your mailman, emptied that dusty bottle of champagne you've been keeping around forever, then what?

The scene shifts now to the next morning, mere seconds after leaving Lottery Headquarters. Your first check has been deposited electronically to your checking account. Now what do you do?

List below everything you plan to do with your winnings in the first year. After taxes, you get about $1.5 million this first year. (Can you manage on that?) Here and on the next page, list absolutely everything you can think of. Everything.

_____

_____

Have you listed *everything?* Have you gone through paying off debts, buying houses and cars for friends and family, squirreling a sizable sum away in the bank? Have you purchased travel tickets, played lots of golf, bought all the software you couldn't afford before (or vitamins or outfits or baubles)? Have you packed your kids off to the finest universities, secured season tickets to the ballet or your favorite pro football team? When we say everything, we mean *everything!*

Once you've imagined everything you might possibly do with your winnings and you just can't imagine anything more, consider this next scenario:

Say it's a Tuesday morning. You've gotten up as usual in your purple mink bathrobe and your gold lamé bed slippers and you've rung one of your maids to hurry up with yet another fabulous breakfast in bed. Ho-hum, salmon soufflé and caviar jelly on toast. Guava juice flown in direct from Tahiti. Coffee delivered personally by Juan Valdez. Whatever do the simple folk do?

An hour later, as you're relaxing by your Olympic-size swimming pool and gazing at the ducks in your personal pond, the one next to your prizewinning rose garden, you ask yourself a question: What am I going to do today?

You're sick of packing and running in and out of hotels and getting on and off your private jet. So travel's out.

Shopping? Please . . . a royal bore. Besides, you've got everything.

Movies, theater, a sporting event? Seen it, done it, been there.

Today you want to do something different. You want to *give* something this time, contribute to the world, take on a challenge. You want to work.

What do you do? What would you want to do? Remember, the sky's the limit—you're filthy rich. All you've got to do is choose it and it's yours. You can choose anything. So choose, already!

In this space, write down anything that comes to mind. Don't be shy; don't worry if it's realistic or attainable to you *now*. Just play along with us. Anything that comes to mind will be just great, thank you. Then resume reading.

Choice 1. Owning a Company

Now on the lines below, write down the names of five actual companies that you'd love to own. Or list five types of companies you might like to own—for example, a dirigible manufacturer, a corn-husking service, a magazine conglomerate, a gourmet coffee shop, a video store. Your choice.

1. _____
2. _____
3. _____
4. _____
5. _____

What companies or types of companies did you choose? Remember, you're the boss. You can choose any kind of company and run it the way you like (within legal limits, of course). Think about why you chose the companies you did. What attracted you to each? Was it the company's product or service? Was it the way the company is run (working conditions, customer service)? Was it the industry the company is in?

On the lines below, summarize the principal elements that attracted you to the companies you chose.

1. _____

_____

2. _____

_____

3. _____

_____

4. _____

_____

5. _____

_____

Choice 2. Going Back to School

Now consider going back to school. Remember, money is no object. In fact, you can't stop laughing when the admissions clerk asks if you'd like a financial aid application. Hardy-har-har! That's a good one, Norton!

On the lines below, write down a list of courses you'd like to take, degrees you'd like to earn. If there are specific schools you might like to attend, jot the names of these schools down as well on the same line as the course or degree program. You'll get into any school you apply for, remember. Money talks.

1. _____

2. _____

3. _____

4. _____

5. _____

What's most important here are the courses and the degree programs you chose. They offer you clues to the type of work you might like to do next. So which courses, which degree programs? What exactly appeals to you about these courses? Do any relate to the companies you chose to buy? Is there any theme or pattern emerging? Which subjects did you choose that simply sound as if they'd be a lot of fun to study? Remember, you don't *need* to work, but you can if you want to. Since you wouldn't be doing it for the money, what kind of work would be just like play?

Below, summarize the reasons you chose these schools and courses of study. Place heavy emphasis on why your chosen studies might be fun.

1. _____

2. _____

3. _____

4. _____

5. _____

Choice 3. Contributing to a Cause

Now consider contributing heavily to a cause. Don't just throw your money around, though. Think about something you could really care about. What kind of a world would you like this to be? What societal problem would you like to solve? What suffering would you like to erase? What kind of boost would you like to give someone?

On the next page, list five causes you would contribute to. Place a figure for the amount of your contribution after the name of each cause or organization. Don't forget to sign the check.

1. _____

2. _____

3. _____

4. _____

5. _____

So who gets your largesse? What causes did you choose? Whatever you decide here could have tremendous impact on the kind of work that would be meaningful to you. It could offer you a personal sense of contribution to the world through your work life. Why should work simply be carrying out other people's orders, other people's visions? What kind of a world do *you* want? Why not implement your values through your work?

Below, summarize your thoughts about the kind of world you want to help create and how you might like to contribute to your vision through your own efforts. Don't worry about the ultimate realizableness of your vision. If we don't try, we have no chance of succeeding. Just think here about what you care about.

1. _____

2. _____

3. _____

4. _____

5. _____

Choice 4. Trading Places With Someone Else

Now how about trading places with someone else in the work world? You can do this if you want to, right? Just bribe somebody to let you do their job for a while. (Everyone has their price, right, Moneybags?) Whom would you choose to trade places with? Whom do you *envy* for the work they do?

On the next page, list five people you'd be excited to trade places with:

1. _____

2. _____

3. _____

4. _____

5. _____

Whom did you choose? Was it people you know personally, or was it people you've observed from afar? What appeals to you about each person's work? Why would having their skills and carrying out their line of work mean so much to you? Summarize your feelings about these questions below.

1. _____

_____

2. _____

_____

3. _____

_____

4. _____

_____

5. _____

_____

Assessing Your Choices

Now review *all* your responses. Look them over and note how they connect with each other, feed off each other, support each other, even contradict each other. If any do contradict each other, could this seeming contradiction be seen in a positive light? How could your contradictions be complementary or combined?

Here's an example: Suppose you notice you're interested in farming. You love all aspects of it—cows, sheep, agriculture, the barns and tractors and farm implements. You also want to work

indoors, however, in a nice cozy office setting, with quiet eleva-
tors and brassy door handles and personal computers. How
could you work on a farm and still go to work every day indoors?

Consider some ideas below. Play around with your
thoughts. Let your imagination run free. Any ideas are valid.
Just consider what kind of options you can come up with that
would accommodate both farming and working indoors.

1. _____

_____

2. _____

_____

3. _____

_____

4. _____

_____

5. _____

_____

Finished brainstorming? We bet you came up with some
pretty wild (and yet feasible) ideas. Here are a few of ours:

- You could work for a government agency such as the Farm
  Bureau.
- You could work in the main headquarters of a large corpo-
  rate farm.
- You could be a field inspector who visits farms from time
  to time but doesn't spend every day on them.
- You could work in a farm museum.
- You could work for a farmers' lobbying group in Wash-
  ington.

Get the way the game is played? At first glance, we don't
always see how our seeming contradictions can be accommo-

dated. But they always can. Our imaginations can be pretty powerful instruments. Use yours today.

"My Work Interests" Mind Map

About time for another mind map, wouldn't you say? With all these new themes, ideas, patterns, clues, directions running around in your head now, you've got to get a handle on them. What better way than a "My Work Interests" Mind Map?

Place the words "My Work Interests" in the center of a sheet of poster paper, or use the space provided in the frame on the next page. Run enough lines or tentacles out from the center to represent all of the categories we've had you review. Remember to spin off any subcategories or ideas for exploring each main category. Add lots of pictures and doodles and connect whatever needs to be connected with dotted lines. You know the drill. This should really get you moving! From here on, it's going to be fun, fun, fun!

＊＊＊

Intermission

Feel free now to get up, stretch, go out to the refrigerator, or take a walk outside. We'll be resuming our action in just a few minutes.

＊＊＊

Hey there, everyone! Good to see you back so refreshed and revitalized. What did you come up with? As before, notice any themes that run through your mind map. What kind of work interests keep coming at you? What kind of conditions do you find you want to work under? What kind of people do you want to work with? Whom do you want to serve as customers or clients, and why? What kind of personal satisfaction will you reap from your work contributions?

Are you coming up with any crystal-clear answers yet? Is anything leaping out at you? If so, congratulations! You've

"My Work Interests" Mind Map

begun to identify the kind of work you'd like to move to. You're way ahead of the game if you can do this now. Good for you!

If, however, your answers are still not quite so clear, don't fret. We're not through yet, not by a long shot. Maybe, though, you can discern a few clues. If so, tuck them away for future reference. Clues, as Detective Columbo or Nancy Drew will attest, are what get us down the road toward a complete solution. And yes, you will get there. Just keep collecting your clues and depositing them in your "My Work Interests" Mind Map. Your understanding of the work you want next will grow and grow. Don't give up the ship.

What's Unique About *You*?

So far, we've been guiding you toward answers that will help you know what new work you might *want* to do. We think that's the best place to start, in contrast to more traditional approaches that begin with what you have thus far demonstrated you *can* do. While it's valuable to be clear about what your skills are—it's certainly part of the mix that defines who you are and what value you hold in the marketplace—such knowledge doesn't assist you much in moving to a new line of work. For that, you've got to know what excites you.

Your demonstrated skills at best represent only a small slice of the potential you carry around with you. They don't speak to your capacity for learning new and different skills, based on your talents and enthusiasm. Focusing only on skills merely traps you in limiting thinking.

That's why you must be cautious when your loved ones, friends, colleagues, even career advisers "wisely" caution you about the long odds of your breaking out of the pink-collar ghetto. They're only trying to help when they say things like:

"It's a tough job market out there."
"You've got to be crazy to leave a good job like this."
"All you're qualified to be is an admin."
"You'd have to start at the bottom if you switched fields."
"Why would anyone hire *you* for a job like that?"

"Maybe you should just try for an executive admin position."

"I wouldn't want to see you get hurt."

It's nice of them to want to help, but the problem is that
such advice doesn't help. For the most part it keeps us focused
on what we've done in the past and not on what we might accomplish in the future. It speaks only to skills and not to potential or undeveloped talent. What they're not heeding is how
frequently these molds get broken and how strong our human
spirit really is.

Though no records are kept on how many people try to
change their careers and how many succeed or fail in the bargain, anecdotes abound that prove it can be done! And each tale
of success points to the abundance of human talent waiting to
be put in motion. You are indeed more than "just an admin" or
"just a secretary." You are so much more.

Talents and Skills Unite!

So let's turn now to your talents as well as your demonstrated
skills. We want to look at the kind of work you *want* to do as
well as how far you've come in showing that you *could* do it.
Your skills, as we've just pointed out, tend to be focused on first
and foremost because they're out there—they've served as living, breathing manifestations of your capabilities. Other talents
may have shown their faces in your work life as well, although
sometimes a job doesn't let us show certain talents, which then
lie quietly inside us, waiting for their big chance. Consequently,
we've got to inventory talent too if we're going to define clearly
all of what's unique about you.

Talents and skills must be seen not as a box to trap you in
but as expansive and versatile facets of yourself, applicable to
many, many situations and needs. Only our inner barriers prevent us from seeing where else our talents and skills can contribute. Our imaginations, in contrast, unlock closed doors.

Listen to a few reflections of successful former admins who

saw the light one day and recognized the transferability of their talents and skills:

Stephanie: "Back when I first learned to type in high school, I didn't see how it could help me beyond secretarial work. That was then; this is now. With computers the name of the game, I'm way ahead of everybody. It got me a promotion and a career switch into the research lab."

Gilda: "I have excellent organizing skills. They served me well as an executive assistant, but now that I'm in account management they save me so much time. I look around at my co-workers and I see them late for appointments, forgetting to return phone calls, losing paperwork. Those kinds of things are the least of my worries. Instead, I get to concentrate on what really needs to be done—watching our client accounts and keeping clients happy!"

Jamie: "I was always good at greeting customers and making them feel comfortable when they visited my reception lobby. Now I do the same thing as a customer service representative, but I get paid a lot more for it. And I've earned such great performance reviews, I'm now being considered for manager of the department! Those days working the reception desk really paid off!"

Patrick: "I was always poring over the company budget with my boss back when I was his assistant. For some reason, I had a knack for seeing details he didn't, and he used to acknowledge me for it. Now I'm a corporate comptroller. Budgets here are more sophisticated than they were back in my admin days, but it's chiefly the same activity. I'm good at it too. I always have been."

Everyone struggles with the notion of "transferable skills" because it's so hard to see ourselves objectively. Yet when we step back and observe what we've gotten acknowledged for, what we've shown a "knack" for, we begin to define our uniqueness.

"Only Me" Collage

"Only Me" Collage

Find a photo of yourself and paste it in the center of a sheet of poster-size paper, or use the space provided in the accompanying frame. Make it one that's all smiles.

Now draw or paste around your photo symbols or pictures that characterize your talents and skills. Figure out what these are by analyzing your daily activities and by studying your professional achievements. What have you found that you are good at? What have you learned to do well? What functions do you perform, even those you don't feel particularly good at? What have you been praised for, rewarded for? What have you learned or accomplished that you never thought you could?

Note here any talents that don't get exercised much (or at all) in your work setting. Maybe these are things that you do well off the job. Maybe you just *think* you'd be good at them if given the chance. Look back at your list of people you envy for their jobs. Do they do things you think you could excel at, if given the chance? Paste or draw these talents and skills in.

Use cut-outs from magazines and newspapers to supplement your imagination. Complete this segment of your collage, then go on to our next instructions.

Enlisting Your Friends and Colleagues

Now let's get a few other brilliant minds into the act. Ask your friends to contribute to your collage. What do they see in you that perhaps you've missed? Are there talents and skills they've observed in you that you haven't depicted? Show them your collage and ask for their comments. Then paste in cut-outs or draw in their ideas.

Next, do the same with colleagues. These are the folks who *really* know how you operate. You may be surprised at how supportive (and delighted) they'll be when you ask for their help. Choose only positive-minded colleagues, however. There's always one ninny in every group who lives for the chance to drag you down into a dark, dank career pit. Stay away from him or her! You want this to stay fun.

Analyzing Your Results

Theoretically you could keep adding to and subtracting from your "Only Me" Collage for the rest of your life. It's a process that doesn't have to end. You're an ever changing masterpiece that keeps growing, learning, achieving. Keep thinking of new things and watching your collage change shape.

But for the moment, let's take stock. What's your first impression here? What kind of a picture have you painted of yourself? What skills and talents are confirmed in your collage? What's here that you hadn't expected to find? Do your talents and skills suggest a usefulness in any career areas that appeal to you? Do your talents and skills suggest career areas you'd never considered before?

On the lines below, make a list of all skills and talents you see in your collage. If you run out of room, keep going on separate sheets of paper. You want to have as clear a picture as you can of what's unique about you. While any one specific skill or talent won't be unique to you, the combination of all of them will be. In the next chapter, we'll investigate career areas you might want to pursue. Along the way, you'll want to refer to this list and collage (which, remember, you can keep adding to). In doing so, you'll pinpoint to what extent you presently display the specific skill set or talent set a desirable career requires.

1. _____

2. _____

3. _____

4. _____

5. _____

6. _____

7. _____

8. _____

9. _____

10. _____

FROM THE ADMIN FILES

Name of ex-admin: Chantal Weaver*

Currently: Field recruitment specialist for TJ Maxx, the nation's leading "off-price" retailer, helping staff new stores nationwide and working with field recruitment managers on their advertising campaigns

Admin skills used today: Talking to people, administrative work, phone work

How change was made: "I'd always been interested in HR and in recruiting, but I didn't know which aspect of it. I took an admin position in the training department at TJ Maxx with the idea of segueing into recruiting."

Chantal's strategy involved conducting lots of career conversations with people in various departments, picking up in particular on relationships she developed from her admin position. "People from other parts of the company had to interact with our department at one time or another."

She also found in her boss, Marg Balcom, then the company's assistant VP of recruiting, an outstanding mentor. When she told Marg what she wanted to do, Marg immediately replied: "OK, let's get started. I want you to schedule one hour a week to meet with me, during which I'll teach you what you need to know to move on."

Says Chantal: "This had never happened to me before. In my previous company, the atmosphere for admins who wanted to move on had been very difficult. You weren't encouraged to explore a new career. Here support made itself available as soon as you asked for it."

Many sessions with Marg and many, many career conversations later, a position opened up in the recruiting department and Chantal was ready for it. She scored high in her interview and got the job.

Best advice to admins: "I highly recommend meeting lots of people and talking to anyone who works in an area you might like to transition into. If your company doesn't encourage it, do it on

*Author's note: After our interview, Chantal advanced her career further by accepting a new position wth Hewlett-Packard.

your own time." She explains that in her previous company she had gotten to know VPs and many others by meeting them for lunch.

She also describes a project she'd initiated at TJ Maxx, a relocation resource guide for new minority hires, that brought her into working contact with the recruiting department: "I put a rough draft together and met with the recruiting department to learn their thoughts. That way they got to see what I could do and I learned more about them."

FROM THE ADMIN FILES

Name of ex-admin: Gwen Champion

Currently: Direct mail manager, Simpson Design, Inc., Tulsa, Oklahoma

Admin skills used today: Coordination of tasks, keeping deadlines, planning and looking ahead to upcoming projects

How change was made: "I'd been feeling for a long time that what I did wasn't all that different from what I'd seen others doing in the companies I worked for. My job might have paid less and received less status, but many of the managers I observed did the same things I did—chatting with people, arranging meetings, making decisions on the spot.

"One day, I told my boss what I'd been feeling. I said I was willing to do whatever it might take to move ahead. I'd go back to school, I'd take on extra projects, whatever.

"She said she'd been waiting for me to come to her and ask for her help. She explained that she saw it to be her job to guide anyone on her staff to new places in their career, but she insisted on waiting for them to initiate it. 'You're not really committed until you say it out loud,' she told me, 'and ask someone for help.'

"After that she introduced me to many people, kept me aware of opportunities in the company, tutored me in how to negotiate for a new position, and encouraged me to go back to school at night (which I did)."

Best advice for admins: "Never be afraid to talk to people about your ambitions. It's easy for admins to feel as though they have no right to *any* ambitions, that they've been selected for this lot in life. You may be afraid, but go ahead anyway. Tell yourself you deserve something better."

5

What Can You Contribute?

It's easy to downplay how valuable we are. It's all too easy too to underrate the skills and expertise we bring to our jobs. We go about our work day to day; we get better and better at it but fail to recognize how much improvement takes place. The ease with which we perform our sometimes complicated, always sophisticated duties replaces our original maze of confusion, awkwardness, and uncertainty. No one compliments us much any more about what we do; no one tells us we're making progress. We just plod along.

For the moment, then, let's kick back and wax philosophic about the role you play. Have you ever thought, for example, about your work in "larger" terms? Have you acknowledged yourself lately for the indispensable contribution you make in your workplace? Can you see how much less effective the whole operation would be without you—you personally—as a part of it?

As an admin, you probably get schizophrenic signals about how valuable you are to your employer. On the one hand, you're told, "I could never afford to lose you," "You're my right arm," and "We could never have done it without you." On the other hand, should you come around asking for a raise, more time off, or greater responsibility, suddenly your bosses and colleagues pull their wagons in a circle. "But you're just a secretary," you hear for the six millionth time. Or how about these: "There's no money in the budget," "Two weeks off is the best we can do." "A lot of girls would love to have your job."

Small wonder then that most admins throw up their hands at the thought of career advancement and resign themselves to a five-day-a-week pressure cooker for the rest of their working lives. Contribution to society? Personal value? Forget about it!

If you want to advance yourself, you've got to hack your way through this thicket of mixed messages and make your way to a clearing. What, in fact, do you *want* to contribute? What kind of a legacy do you *want* to leave behind? Is there something about who you are and what you do for others that's especially meaningful to you?

Dreaming of Retirement

To people who love their work, dreams of retirement never enter the picture. When people believe in what they do, when they feel that the world gains great value from their career contributions, they scorn retirement. Not doing what they do would be more stressful than doing it.

Take George Burns, for example. When he was eighty-five, he announced he'd just signed a five-year contract with Caesar's Palace in Las Vegas. "Imagine that," he said. "Five years! Imagine me signing a contract of that length of time with anybody!" After his customary puff on his cigar, he dropped his punch line, "Normally I never sign a contract for less than ten!"

George Burns has never understood why people retire. He loves what he does, seeing the effect it makes on his audiences nightly. He clearly knows his contribution.

Whom else can we cite? How about Bob Hope, Billy Graham, Jimmy Carter, Lionel Hampton, and Mother Theresa? Or the late Linus Pauling, Jessica Tandy, Buckminster Fuller? We keep on working whenever we see clearly our impact on others' lives. It makes our work worth the trouble.

As an experiment, let's suppose you are heading for your retirement party. Let's imagine that you're being driven in a limousine toward the big event all decked out in your finest threads and licking your lips at the thought of tonight's sumptuous feast and the presents amassing on a gift table. Hundreds of guests will bustle about, eager to honor you.

It's going to be a swell time, you can bet on it, but as you settle back in your limo, you begin to wonder what the speakers tonight are going to say. Oh, you know they'll have great things to recall about you. They'll toast you and tell everyone how great you are. But *what* exactly will they say?

You watch the trees outside glowing in the twilight as you begin thinking about what you'd like the speakers to say. You're thinking about what you've tried to do in your life and the effect you've tried to have. After a while, you've got it pretty well set in your mind how you'd like to be remembered.

How Would You Like to Be Remembered?

Here and on the next page, jot down a few tributes you'd like to hear about yourself during speeches at your retirement party. Keep in mind these questions. Use a separate sheet of paper if you'd like to list more.

1. What kind of an impact have you tried to have on people's lives? _____

_____

_____

2. What specific contribution do you want to be remembered for?

_____

_____

_____

3. In what ways have you tried to improve the order of things?

_____

_____

_____

4. What value have you tried to add to the way things have always been? _____

_____

_____

5. What problems have you most tried to solve? _____

_____

_____

The Arrival of "The Job"

Now that you've thought about your skills, talents, and contributions, it's time to consider constructing a "partnership." In the work world, the concept of partnership is an old one insofar as it is considered an arrangement between individual entities of equal stature. It has, however, lain dormant throughout much of this century as corporate hierarchies have developed and stratified the work world. Yet seeing yourself as equal to whomever you might next work for or with will be crucial to seeing yourself as someone whose uniqueness can stay powerful and continually marketable.

In the olden days (the *very* olden days), partnerships were more common. Workers plied their trade with others of similar economic means and social position. Farmer, tinsmith, blacksmith, weaver—whatever your station—you generally ran your own business, sold goods or services to a variety of clientele in the town and countryside, and purchased or traded goods and services with those who provided something you couldn't supply for yourself. Though kings and lords dwelled hither and yon, for the most part people engaged in commerce in a spirit of equality within the same general economic class. Because most people's labor was so visible, so down-to-earth, they, of course, could also see clearly how their work contributed to the general welfare.

Somewhere along the way came "The Job." It all started out innocently enough—a little machine shop here, a crafts cooperative there. Somehow, though, as the nineteenth century cranked itself into a frenzy, workplaces began to get bigger and more strong bodies were needed to haul objects, fit pieces of things together, screw on bolts, and then repeat all these tasks over and over and over from morning till dusk, day after day.

People began to migrate, too. The predominant work model became a Monday-through-Friday (or Saturday), forty-plus-hours-per-week, fifty-weeks-per-year "job" slot, compensated with a "living wage" (in contrast with the old idea of a fee for services) and two or three weeks' "vacation" (which used to be taken whenever one wanted, throughout the year). Some job slots even offered "benefits" such as health care, a retirement plan, and life insurance.

What at first glance might have seemed progress, however, insidiously stole a great deal away. As individual workers were placed into narrow job slots, they suffered a disconnection with what their work really meant. They stopped experiencing the satisfaction of the customer at the end of the line. In the auto industry, for example, a worker might drill a hole into one corner of a car's chassis for eight or nine hours each day, five and a half days a week, fifty weeks a year. This could go on year after year, decade after decade. "What do you do?" an auto worker would find himself being asked at a social gathering or on the street. He'd likely have two potential responses: "I drill holes" or "I work for General Motors." Never: "I make cars." He didn't make cars, at least not in his own mind. He might see them driving along the road, but that was a far cry from the hole-drilling duties he performed every day.

It's not surprising, then, that this disconnection would be felt by today's admins too. As the profession of administrative assistant has gotten more and more specialized, many admins find themselves unsure of where they fit in, of what the impact of their day-to-day duties really is. When people are just doing a "job"—that is, a series of tasks defined by someone else—rather than directly affecting an end result, (customers), they come to feel like replaceable cogs in a gigantic machine. They certainly don't see themselves as equal partners.

THE DISCONNECTION DILEMMA

Consider the case of Joanie, an administrative assistant with a large research firm. Joanie spends her days typing up research reports on studies of chemical spills, environmental hazards, recycling plants. Although she inputs these reports into large databases, someone else analyzes them and an administrative assistant in another wing of the building inputs the results of that analysis.

Final reports go out to the client company, generally a big government agency where another staff of analysts think about them, put together their reactions, and then have a pool of their own admins input this new report into yet another computer. Somewhere down the line a report based on all this analysis, reactive analysis, and reactive reactive analysis gets delivered to the President of the United States, or the secretary of the interior, or the undersecretary of the interior, or maybe to the State Department or to the Environmental Protection Agency. Basically Joanie has no idea where it all ends up, and long ago she gave up caring.

"Say, Joanie," we holler, "what do you do for a living?"

"I type research reports into a computer all day, that's all." Hey, what else can she tell us?

Partnerships to the Rescue

There's a way out of this "disconnection dilemma," so stay with us; we're leading you there. If you keep looking inside yourself, defining not only your skills, talents, and abilities but your passions and contributions, you can create partnerships in your work life similar to those that existed before the Age of Jobs. Once you do that, you'll find yourself in touch with the meaning and impact of your work contributions and thus experience more genuine satisfaction from what you do.

In order to achieve this, you've got to now go beyond defining your own uniqueness and next identify who wants or needs it. With whom can you partner to create a win-win economic exchange? Who has a problem that *you* can solve? How can you peddle your newly ID'd skills and talents so that each of you in this partnership wins, that is, so you'll find yourself with work that's meaningful, challenging, lucrative, and enjoyable and your partner will gain a service that advances his, her, or its goals?

You may have to break the bounds of convention, perhaps

even the way you've been brought up. Our parents, after all, were all born and raised in the Age of Jobs. That means they became acculturated to attitudes and behaviors associated with how to be a successful employee. Many of these run counter to how to be a successful "partner." So we've got to learn new ways to think and act.

To help you recondition yourself, consider the following statements made by professionals in today's work world. Which seem in tune with the principles of work-world partnership, and which with being a good employee? Record your answer by checking the appropriate box.

Harriet: "I know what I'm supposed to do each day. That's one good thing about where I work. My boss always has it clearly laid out for me—packaging mail, upgrading the software, rechecking correspondence. He's extremely well organized."

Employee? ☐   *Partner?* ☐

Debby: "I'm constantly on the lookout for new projects, new things I can learn from. It doesn't take much extra effort to find them either. I just keep asking people, 'How can I help you?' and they tell me!"

Employee? ☐   *Partner?* ☐

Sue Ellen: "I've got this idea for a new way to greet company visitors. Instead of just having them sign in at the reception desk, we could hand them a company brochure and offer them coffee while they wait. We could spread goodwill and promote ourselves while we make them a little more comfortable. I've already suggested this to our operations manager."

Employee? ☐   *Partner?* ☐

Thelma: "I know I'm good at what I do. I work overtime, take work home, do personal errands for my boss. I go way beyond what's expected. So where are those two extra personal days I've seen other people on my level get? And why am I not being given more responsibility and authority? I think it may be time to speak to the union about all this."

      Employee? ☐   *Partner?* ☐

Alexandra: "I've been wanting to move up from my job for a long time. I work in a financial investments company. My goal is to become a certified financial planner. I started as a temp three years ago, mostly as a filing assistant, but I've been taking courses at night in financial planning and I never miss a guest speaker at lunch or a chance to sit down with one of the investment counselors and pick their brains. I feel confident I can be a very good planner. I've just got to convince someone to let me into the training program."

      Employee? ☐   *Partner?* ☐

Lucy: "Well, I like that! How dare they? I put in for a transfer to go from the accounting department to the marketing department six months ago, and now I see they've hired twelve new people, all from the outside. After I submitted that application I never heard another word. I don't think there's a chance in hell for someone like me to advance in this company. It's hopeless."

      Employee? ☐   *Partner?* ☐

The answers to this exercise are pretty obvious. We tried to make them that way because we were more interested in making clear the contrast between an employee mentality and a partner mentality than in tripping you up! So we'll score all of you an A on this latest quiz.

As you can see, the employee tends to be passive and willing to follow orders and just do what's expected (like Harriet). When she does go beyond minimal expectations, she does things like fill out applications and follow "proper" procedures, and then she faults other individuals or the entire system when no one notices (Lucy). She refuses to take risks and feels justified in not doing so. The rationale seems to be that as long as she's doing what she's been told to do, she ought to be taken care of (Thelma). The employee attitude is one of entitlement.

A partner, instead, intuitively knows that no one's going to take care of her. She sees that to succeed and advance she has to get herself noticed by initiating ideas and going out and finding someone in authority who'll pay attention (Debby, Sue Ellen, and Alexandra). No one's going to make it easy for her; she just has to believe in what she's doing and risk rejection.

A partner's idea might be to contribute an improvement to a current system, like greeting visitors in the reception lobby (Sue Ellen), or it might be more personal, such as getting enrolled in a company training program (Alexandra). A partner also appreciates the value of helping out by asking colleagues what they need (Debby), then getting involved in whatever challenges that will give her the chance to grow. She enhances her professional value in the marketplace by this behavior and affords decision makers an opportunity to see what she can do.

How to Be the Perfect Partner

In business, everyone's always looking for a perfect match. Where can we find customers who want our product or service? Does your resumé match the job requirements spelled out in that help wanted ad? How do two business partners complement each other—that is, do their individual skills and temperaments add up to a good team?

You must also look for a match when exploring new directions. What problems or needs have been waiting for someone to come along and help with them? When you find one, you'll next want to ask, "Could that 'someone' be me?"

In the Chinese written language, the symbol for *crisis* also signifies *opportunity*. That is the way you want to be thinking when you scurry about in search of your match. Specifically, ask yourself these questions:

"What problems at my place of work need to be solved?"
"What projects have been on hold, waiting for someone to help get them started?
"What new ideas could dramatically improve profits and customer relations?"

"What new systems could be implemented that would speed up service and/or cut costs?"

These questions should give you the general idea. Any help you can offer your company or a department or manager that would improve the way things are currently done, or increase business, or solve a major problem, or fill a need, or get something started may be an "opportunity match" waiting to happen. A decision-maker gets busy at work and doesn't always have the time or energy to pay attention to everything that needs to be done. His or her secret prayer is that someone will suddenly come along and offer competent assistance and a sack full of fresh ideas. That's where you come in.

FINDING THAT PERFECT MATCH

One day, Sharon Casey, an admin for the VP of operations at a biotech firm in South Carolina, finds herself sitting at lunch with the company's lab technicians. Before long, she's lunching with them two or three times a week and talking with them about the work they do. After about a month of this, Sharon realizes she's been really looking forward to these lunches and that she never tires of hearing about projects, adventures, and the mishaps of life in the lab.

She begins to wonder about transferring there. At first, she figures all she can hope for is administrative work, same as she is doing now. But Phyllis and Kate are the lab's two admins, and they don't seem to be planning on leaving anytime soon.

One day at lunch, one of the technicians mentions a research project he's been wanting to get funded for a long time. He feels certain that his idea meets all the criteria required by the pertinent government agency, but he's been so swamped lately he hasn't been able to complete the paperwork.

Boing! Sharon has a brainstorm.

"Tim," she begins, taking him aside. "I think I might be able to help. What if I worked with you to complete the paperwork? I'm sure if you just showed me how to fill in the forms I could do most of it for you. We could get enough of your proposal in shape so you could finally submit it for funding."

Tim has been looking for the time to spend on this for some months now, not to mention someone who could type and make sense of the complicated government forms. Sharon's offer is a dream come true. "I really appreciate this," he says. "Yes, of course, I'll accept your help. But, Sharon, may I ask why you would be doing this? It's only going to cost you more time and trouble on your end."

Sharon has a clear response. "Tim, I've been lunching with you and your coworkers for over a month now, and I can't believe how fascinated I've become with what you all do. In fact, it's gotten me more interested in what the whole company does. Last week I read our annual report cover to cover, and I've even begun subscribing to a couple of industry trade magazines. I sometimes imagine myself working in the research department because it sounds like so much fun. I guess what I'm saying is this: If you ever hear of any position in the lab that I might qualify for, I'd love to be considered for it."

Tim thinks for a moment and then says, "You know, if this funding comes through for me, I'll need a research assistant." Butterflies begin bumping up against the walls of Sharon's stomach. "You might need to do some admin work for me," he continued, "but there'd definitely be lab work I'd need help with too, which you could learn."

Sharon had found her perfect match. She'd hung out with folks who interested her, begun reading and learning more about the work they did, and kept her ears open. Once she heard about a problem she could help with, she volunteered her services. Then she made known her personal goals. By that point, her new partner, Tim, had become more than willing to help her out.

Now, we know what some of you may be saying (especially the "employee-minded"): "Hey, Ken and Barbara, this all sounds great, but scenarios like this come along once in a lifetime. Real life is much less generous."

Is this really a one-in-a-million scenario? Is it unlikely you would ever run across a similar situation in your life? Was Sharon Casey merely lucky? The answers to all three questions are no. Scenarios similar to this one have happened to many, many of our clients. Most of them, by the way, also started out disbelieving something like this could happen to them; yet, after they got their career advancement campaign in gear, something like it eventually did.

However, by way of paying slight homage to your skepticism, let us add the following: Although this kind of scene *can* play itself out as easily as we've depicted, and although it will do so much more often than you might think, never, never, never *expect* it to. You see, expectation tends to foster passive frames of mind. We sometimes get a little too comfortable when we expect something will happen. We don't try as hard, do as much. If you don't believe us, check out the dictionary definition of the word *expect*. Among the entries you'll find "to wait," "await," and "to consider probable or certain."

When it comes to career advancement, you've got to put out an effort of 100—no, make that 1000—percent! There are so many potential forks in the road, ruts, fallen rocks, discouraging words. You can't let your guard down for one minute! Passivity has no place, nor does waiting, feeling overconfident, or getting too comfortable.

Instead follow the steps Sharon Casey took:

1. *Observe.* What do you notice that's not working well in your company? What could be improved? You don't have to have all the answers in hand at first. You just need to develop a knack for spotting problems.

2. *Locate who's in charge of the problem.* Sharon heard Tim grousing about a project he couldn't find time to get off the ground. His project sounded like it needed a skill (help with paperwork) she could offer him. That was her cue.

3. *Decide if there's a role you genuinely want to play.* If there is, make your wants public. If Sharon had heard of a similar need in the accounting or the marketing department, would she have volunteered to help there too? Probably not. Her excitement was focused on the research lab. That's the place she wanted to end up. Tim's need for her help offered the opening to get her there.

Sniffing Out Trouble

There's a cardiothoracic surgeon at one of New York City's major hospitals who's become renowned around his operating room for sniffing out trouble. Many times he'll ask a staff physician or nurse about a matter that doesn't feel right to him, then sense that the staffer is unable to discover the problem. On such occasions, Dr. Bob mutters, "There's something wrong around here and I'm going to find out what it is." Then he proceeds to do so.

You should emulate this surgical bloodhound. Fortunately, for us and the world in general, there are always problems. There's an abundance of needs to fill and there always will be. That's why you can feel confident a career match is in your future. You just have to look for it.

On the next page, put together a new mind map focusing on how your company is doing. You can include good things your company is doing if that will help get the juices flowing, but don't forget to include any problems, needs, or crises that come to mind. Write your company's name in the center and branch out with your wavy lines and tentacles as you did in previous mind maps. Just see what you come up with.

[*Note:* If you are thinking of moving to another company, or if you are unemployed and targeting a number of companies, use only one of these companies for this exercise. To use them all might make the mind map too complicated and confusing.]

Read

Your next step is to read. Get hold of the company annual report, the company press kit, the company newsletter—any information that the company publishes about itself. Read this material thoroughly. Take notes as you read. Notice those areas the company is involved in that interest you. Ask yourself if you could imagine working on this or that project, or in such and such a department.

Next, get a little critical. Do you agree with everything you're reading? Do you disagree with anything the company is doing, or the way it's doing it? Can you spot any flaws in the company's thinking or strategy? Did you notice any missing pieces? Put the whole company under your microscope.

Go back and add your latest thoughts and ideas to your mind map.

"Company Evaluation" Mind Map

More Stuff to Read

In addition to whatever printed materials you can get from the company, hustle down to your local library and see what you can find there. Look up books and magazine articles not only on your company but on your industry, on similar companies, and on the field or profession you're becoming interested in. If you're not sure how to find all of this, step right up to the reference desk at your library. Tell the reference librarian sitting there that you're doing some career exploration and you need some help getting started. Before long, that reference librarian will become one of your best friends. Don't forget to send her a fruitcake around the holidays.

To supplement library research, be sure to regularly cruise magazine stands and bookstores. Libraries won't always have all the best periodicals or all the latest books on a subject. Keep au courant by doing your own advance work. You might end up suggesting to your reference librarian other materials her library really ought to have. She'll thank you for it.

And one other point of information: In these high-tech times we must pay attention to the emerging technologies that allow us to bring libraries and bookstores right into our homes. If you're hooked up to an "on-line service" (America Online, Prodigy, or Compuserve, to name the better known), you'll find articles available there that you can read on-screen and even print out for your files. These can save a great deal of running-around time, obviously a welcome benefit since in your regular admin life you probably do enough running around as it is.

Now go back and add to your mind map any plans you have for library-type research. Then, after you have implemented your plans, note relevant findings from your research and add these too to your mind map. This thing is really gonna grow!

Career Conversations

Most books on career exploration use the term *informational interview* to indicate a technique for learning more about an intriguing job, career, company, or industry. Informational interviews typically denote one-on-one question-and-answer sessions, usually conducted in person at a formally appointed time. The interviewer, either a potential career changer or a job seeker, asks the questions. The interviewee, usually a manager or other expert or a decision-maker, patiently answers.

Informational interviews typically take place in the interviewee's office for about thirty minutes (or longer if the interviewee gets on a roll), and when it's all over both shake hands and the interviewer leaves. The really conscientious interviewers mail thank-you notes within a day or two. Most of the time, after that, the two never see or hear from each other again.

Want our opinion of this process? Three words: *We hate it!* Not the process exactly, more the form it's conducted in. Here's why:

Informational interviews tend to limit, not enhance, your chance to build valuable career relationships. They are, in our opinion, constricting, limiting, and boxy. They set up a dynamic between both parties that tends to stunt continued growth: "OK, you got what you want; good luck to ya!" That might as well be what the interviewee hears when she leaves the interviewer's office, because that's usually the attitude.

The other problem with informational interviews is that too many people are out there doing them! Many professionals thus get bombarded with requests for them and end up formulating canned rejections so that they won't find themselves giving away too much precious time. Voicing your request by specifically using the word "information interview" raises a red flag and sets such rejection in motion.

As an alternative to the informational interview, we prefer what we call the "career conversation." Can you see a difference, simply in the tone of each label? Informational interviews—bad! Career conversations—good!

How would you compare these two techniques? What does the name of each imply? Why do you suppose we feel so strongly that a career conversation would have it all over the so much better-known informational interview?

In the column below, record your ideas by checking off which technique seems to better fit the characteristic cited. Keep in mind the very sound of each technique's name as you deliberate your answers.

	Informational Interview	*Career Conversation*
Conducted frequently on neutral ground	_____	_____
Two-way communication	_____	_____
Could be loose time frame	_____	_____
Generally by appointment only	_____	_____
Communication very formal	_____	_____
Generally on unfamiliar territory	_____	_____

If you checked the lines under Career Conversation for the first three and the lines under Informational Interview for the bottom three, then you were thinking what we were thinking. You read our minds! To us, career conversations offer much more latitude for getting to know someone, since you could be conducting one off-the-cuff virtually anywhere—at a social gathering, at a professional event, in the supermarket, on the sidewalk outside the post office. Good communication is a two-way street—you talk, they talk, you talk again, they talk some more. There's a loose time frame, too—your talking together ends when it ends, when it's time to end. Everybody acts natural.

Informational interviews, on the other hand, feel just as the title implies: stiff, formal, clinical. You meet on alien turf, which helps you get to know your interviewee's surroundings but also sets up an unequal dynamic for you. It's as if you're this poor, work-world waif. You go out and meet people in *their* offices; they never come to yours. Communication is often set up in a very rigid format—you question the big expert and he deigns to answer you. Within a limited time frame, of course ("I can give you twenty minutes, OK?"); his time is limited. (But you can't help thinking: "And what—mine's not?")

An informational interview is so often set up on such uneven terms that it's bound to foster a lower self-image on your part. That's of course the last thing you need as you work to keep your spirits and optimism up during your career explorations. Instead, what you want to feel is the equal of other professionals. You want to feel that they're not lords or ladies on high, but colleagues, teammates, and working stiffs just like you: potential partners.

Would you call Sharon's exchange with Tim an I or a C? It was obviously a C all the way! In fact, since she'd been lunching with Tim and his colleagues for months, Sharon had been having rounds and rounds of career conversations with them for all that time. What better way to get to know not only the information you're seeking from informational interviews but the professionals themselves as well?

You've got to build your relationships with people as you gather your information, as Sharon had. By the time Tim's time problems came to light during their lunch conversations, Sharon's own competence had become firmly established in Tim's eyes. Can you imagine how different the exchange might have been had Sharon experienced only a brief, stiff, twenty-minute informational interview with Tim five or six months before? Can you imagine?

Sharon is speaking to Tim over the phone:

Sharon: Maybe you don't remember me, but we met five months ago in your office. For an informational interview.

Tim: Um, hmmm. I can't remember exactly. What can I do for you?

Sharon: Well, I, uh, I heard you might be looking for a research assistant sometime soon and I wanted to apply for the job.

Tim: What kind of experience do you have working in a lab?

Sharon: Well, uh, none really. I'm an administrative assistant over here in operations. But I'm very willing to learn. I'm very interested!

Tim: Well, you know the funding hasn't come through yet, and I don't know when it will. But if you send your resumé over to Human Resources, they'll hold it for me.

Sharon: Yes, well, I'll do that. I appreciate your talking to me. Thank you very much for your time. I'll send my resumé out today.

Does the phrase *snowball's chance in hell* come to mind at all?

Look for ways to get to know people, to *really* get to know them. Combine your research techniques with less formalized relationship building. You want people to remember you, to understand what you can do for them, to be willing to take a chance on you. If you rely on more-distant, -impersonalized methods, you'll continually have trouble closing the gap.

"Never Feel Trapped as an Admin"

A "Q and A" With Ethel Cook

Principal of Corporate Improvement Group, located in Bedford, Massachusetts, Ethel Cook is a professional organizer, trainer, consultant, and motivational speaker. Ethel, who was an admin for many years, focuses her consulting practice on teaching admins how to work more effectively as well as how to advance their careers. She conducts a seminar called "Management Skills for Executive Secretaries and Administrative Assistants" for the American Management Association.

Barbara Litwak: How has the job of administrative assistant changed over the last ten years?

Ethel Cook: In the past, admins ran around typing, doing errands, answering the phones, filing. They still do all of that, but now they do a lot more. Much admin work today is project-oriented—writing reports, creating spreadsheets, analyzing demographics, preparing presentations, doing publicity. Admins are the way middle managers used to be.

B.L.: That sounds as if it could open a lot of doors.

E.C.: If you bother to educate yourself, you can really become an expert, especially in areas that are new. For example, if you make it a point to learn all you can about new technologies—software programs, the Internet, phone systems—you can become the company resource person. Everybody will be calling on you! That may justify your being given that role as a job, elevating you from admin status. You can make a proposal that the job of "resource officer" be created and that *you* should fill it.

B.L.: How did you move from admin work to the work you do now?

E.C.: I kept getting bored with admin work. I was always looking for ways to make the job more stimulating. So I started trying to help people. My motto was, "How can I help you?" That got me to make a connection between what others needed done and how I could fit in. One day I found myself teaching people how to file, how to organize their offices. I did it as an employee then. Now I get paid a hefty fee.

B.L.: Sounds as if your transition went pretty smoothly.

E.C.: Not at all! It took a lot of personal growth, as well as networking, to get where I am today. I speak for a living now, but I couldn't do it at all then. I just didn't have high enough self-esteem. But once you start down a road, you have a tendency to keep going.

B.L.: What's the number-one strategy admins should employ to advance themselves?

E.C.: Do what I did: Find a way to fill someone's need, especially that of your boss or someone else in authority. You'll develop new skills and people will get to see what you can do.

I once had a boss who was having a lot of trouble dealing with two other secretaries in his office. They tended to be hard personalities, very confrontational. I went to him and said, "If you don't want to deal with them, I'll do it for you. Just have them go through me." I learned a lot after that about negotiation skills, and it made me the most valuable admin there.

B.L.: What about when your boss doesn't want your help?

E.C.: It does happen. I worked for a manager one time who didn't even want to have contact with me or his other admins, let alone any extra help. I asked him once how I was doing and he told me: "I don't want you to ask me any questions directly. Put your questions on paper. If I choose to answer them, I will. If I don't want to answer you, I won't." Then he said, "And I don't want you to follow up with me either." Brrrr.

When you run up against a boss who won't let you help him with extra projects and obviously isn't going to support you in your career advancement, look around for someone else. At one place I worked, my boss wouldn't spend the time to mentor me. *His* boss, though, needed help on some things, so I offered my services. I started getting some real plum assignments from that, which expanded the breadth of what I knew about and could do. You must never feel trapped as an admin, because you're really not. Whenever you feel that way, remember it's all in your head.

B.L.: What should you ask for in return for helping out others in the company? What will ensure that you'll advance?

E.C.: Training. Education. Learning things. If you're in a small company, take advantage of the need for everyone to wear a lot of hats. Take on other jobs. If you're at a larger company, interact with people in other departments, and not just with the other admins. Look around for people who respect you. Be flexible, cooperative, a team player. Stay away from gossip circles and avoid National Secretaries Day.

B.L.: National Secretaries Day?

E.C.: I believe National Secretaries Day should be abolished. Admins and secretaries are professionals. Why are they being singled out for a special day? Do we have National Engineers Day? Or National Managers Day? This only keeps alive the idea of the pink-collar ghetto. It's like that old commercial: "Promise her anything but give her Arpège." Admins don't need flowers or an annual free lunch; they need training, education, and genuine opportunities.

Treat your admin like a professional is what I say. Remember: Flowers die, lunch gets digested, but learning stays with you forever.

FROM THE ADMIN FILES

Name of ex-admin: Marcia Miller

Currently: President of her own firm, Desktop Design and Publication, a Lexington, Massachusetts, provider of training and documentation materials, product manuals, and Internet site design

Admin skills used today: Typing, office management

How change was made: "I had taken a typing course, which helped get me a job as an office manager for a small engineering firm. As it turned out I didn't do a whole lot of typing because the company really needed someone to organize the office and keep it running. I'd heard about the job through a friend who worked at the company.

"I was more fortunate than a lot of admins or secretaries in that I also had a college degree; and even better for me, it was in science. So I was really overqualified for this job, a fact that became quickly obvious. So I moved up the ranks in a very short time, first filling out various HR functions that needed to be done, then going on to the position of marketing manager. When a big project in Saudi Arabia came up, I took over the project's administration. That solidified the momentum of my career, and I never went back to admin work again."

Best advice for admins: "Work in a small company. You'll wear many hats there, so it's a great way to gain many different kinds of skills."

6

Positioning Your New Self for Success

You've got to be careful. There are those who will help you and those who will not. Professionals in every corner of the work world encounter the tendency of others to pigeonhole:

> "You're an engineer, you say. What could you possibly know about advertising?"
> "You're in advertising, you say. What could you possibly know about training and development?"
> "You're in training and development, you say. What could you possibly know about finance?"
> "You're in finance, you say. What could you possibly know about engineering?"
> "You're an administrative assistant, you say. What could you possibly know about . . . *anything*?"

Our society often views admins as flunkies, automatons, empty-headed drones. It's a job, many assume, that anyone can do. It's just not that hard.

This, when, taken to the extreme, can get downright degrading. You're not even held in the same regard as other adults, as Barbara once learned.

While working at the prestigious Kennedy School of Government at Harvard University as an admin to an environmental consultant, Barbara became friendly with a professor in another department who seemed to value her wit and professionalism, and they talked

frequently about K-School issues and also about world issues, politics, life in general. They seemed to strike up a pretty good rapport.

One day this professor called Barbara to his office to discuss
something "in confidence." Barbara had been looking for a new
opportunity, since her current position seemed to have reached a
plateau, and her professor friend knew it. Maybe he was going to
offer her something.

Barbara settled into a chair in the professor's office, and he got
right to it. "My wife and I are going out of town next month for a
couple of weeks," he began. "I've observed that you seem to be
responsible and conscientious. Would you consider watching our
house and minding our fourteen-year-old daughter while we're
gone?"

Dumbfounded, but discreet, Barbara politely refused with an
excuse about being away herself during that time. But inside, she
both raged and despaired. Was that all he saw her as—a babysitter?

Your image as an admin, then, has to be dealt with every
day. As you begin to build your career relationships, you can't
be too careful about ensuring that you're seen the way you want
to be seen. Stereotypical thinking runs deep. You must always
aggressively clarify what you can do and what you're looking
for. Take no prisoners. Even your very best allies may *want* to
help, but not know how. It's your job to show them.

Leading Your Allies

When we say it's your job to show people what you can do, we
mean you often have to literally lead them. Demonstrate to them
what they can do for you, then shout it to the rafters. "Do you
understand what it is I really do?" may be one early question to
ask any potential ally. Should they say yes, ask them to articulate
it. Very likely, no matter what they say, they won't know how to
paint your abilities and potential in as attractive or marketable a
way as you could. It's your job to help them out, as Marisa has
to do.

THE EDUCATION OF AN ALLY

Marisa has been working in a major manufacturing plant in Virginia. As she begins exploring options inside her company, she finds herself interested in the inspection department. The idea of checking product samples before they're shipped intrigues her, and she also enjoys the camaraderie she observes in the department. The increase in pay for working there appeals to her as well.

Marisa makes lunch plans with Merle, the department's chief inspector. Although Merle has no authority to hire her, Marisa feels that talking with him may give her a clearer idea about what qualifications the department manager is seeking in a new inspector. She gets Merle to accept her invitation to lunch simply by being honest.

"I'm interested in learning more about your department," she tells him. "I'm curious about possible career opportunities, and since you've been there the longest, I'd like to ask you a few questions over lunch. My treat."

Merle's first response is that he doesn't think there are any openings in the department at the present time. Besides, he doesn't handle the hiring himself.

"That's OK," Marisa responds. "I'm not looking to apply right yet. I just want to learn more."

"OK," says Merle. "How about tomorrow at eleven-thirty in the cafeteria?"

The next day, as they sit down to lunch, Marisa again summarizes for Merle why she wants to meet with him. As is often the case when potential career allies are first approached for help, Merle assumes that Marisa is ready to apply for a job. He also assumes that she is seeking another admin position.

"You know, I'd like to help, I really would," he drawls in his Georgia accent, "but to be honest I don't think our department's secretary will be leaving anytime soon. She's been with us thirty-five years, and she tells me she's hanging on for her retirement. That's about five years from now."

[*Time for Marisa to educate Merle, again. Merle, like most potential allies, needs her to explain her intentions two or three times before he'll get it. That's because Marisa's request is not the usual, straightforward "Can you get me a job?" but rather an appeal for Merle's opinions and guidance. Applying for a job comes later.*]

"Merle," she begins carefully, "what I'm actually interested in is leaving my work as an administrative assistant and doing something else. I've been investigating lots of options recently. The inspection department has come to interest me the most. Who knows? Maybe I'll become an inspector someday, like you!"

Merle stabs at a forkful of salad and shovels it into his mouth. Chuckling a little nervously, he says, "With all due respect, Marisa, I don't know if this would be the right job for you. You see, there's not a lot of typing to do when you're an inspector like me. You've got to pay attention to tiny details and have great eyesight. You're always searching for defects in the material. You've also got to move lickety-split when a shipment is ready to go out. That requires an awful lot of finger dexterity so you can pluck out the bad stuff at a moment's notice. Can you see that you might not have the right skills for this line of work?"

[*Notice how Merle has pigeonholed Marisa by the admin work she does now. He doesn't mean to; he is just calling it as he sees it. In fact, he'd probably be the first to say that he himself wasn't qualified for much else than inspection work. It's as if the skills and talents we utilize in our current jobs couldn't possibly be transferred to any other line of work. Fortunately, Marisa had spent oodles of time listening to us, so she knows what to do next.*]

"Merle," she asks, "do you know what I do?"

"Well," Merle replies confidently, "I think I do. If I understand it right, you type letters, answer lots of phone calls, and take a fair amount of dictation. And from what I've seen when I've been down at your office, you're darn good at it too."

"Thanks, Merle," Marisa says. "I've always appreciated a nice compliment."

"Not at all. Just being honest."

"But though you're correct—I do type letters, answer tons of phone calls, and take a little dictation—I also do some of the same things you do in the inspection room."

Even though he's hard at work on his entrée now, Merle is still listening. "How so?" he wonders aloud.

"Well, think of it like this: Whenever I type a letter, I'm paying attention to tiny details, just as you do in your inspection work. I've also got to have a good pair of eyes so I can find typos and other errors on these letters, not to mention that my finger dexterity needs to be right up there with the best of them so that I can type fast, collate reports, and operate calculators, postage machines, and copiers." She pauses to let all this sink in, then finishes with, "And as for moving *fast*, I'm like a wild tornado when a call comes down from the president's office for a copy of one of our reports or something. Believe me, when the president's office calls, it's all hands on deck! Taking your time just doesn't cut it."

Merle is impressed. "Hadn't thought of it that way," he says, swigging the last of his diet soda. "Y'know I can't say if I'd be able to do the work you do—it sounds pretty specialized the way you tell it—but if you want my opinion, I'd say that with a little bit of training and some more practice, you'd do real fine down in the inspection area! Why don't you come over some afternoon and I'll show you around. I'll introduce you to the boss too. He's been thinking about adding on a few trainees in the next month or two."

See how you can't take anyone's understanding of what you do for granted? In the same regard, you certainly can't take for granted the notion that other people can automatically envision your value to them. It's great when it happens on its own—that someone spots you or discovers you—but our advice is, never plan on it. Instead, you must carefully, methodically, patiently lead your allies through the quagmire of trying to see you as the valuable, evolving professional you are. Your image as an admin by no means represents all you can do.

Leading HR

You won't necessarily have an easier time explaining yourself to human resources, but you should plan to utilize them anyway. They usually know of present and future openings in the company. Still, you'll have to work with them the same way as you do when you're building your other career allies. HR folks are trained to think in terms of demonstrated skills and previous work histories, so your proposal to take on some new challenge in the organization may still fall on perplexed ears. Merle's reactions in many ways echoed those of the most seasoned HR pro. What's worse, HR will want to look at your resumé, which often encapsulates your professional credentials in a way you'd rather not display. Your resumé sends the HR specialists zipping about through your past while you'd prefer them to help you in opening up your future.

It might be of value to you, then, to take a moment and think about how you might explain your "transferability" to HR. Why would your particular admin skills be a "plus" in a new career area? You can refer back to Marisa's explanations to Merle. She cited, for example, her skill with typing as a plus in the inspection department because it showed her careful attention to details.

Use a new career direction (NCD) you've begun to think about as a guide for the following exercise. If you're still considering a number of new directions, choose one at random and use that. You'll of course need at least a rudimentary understanding of the skills and talents your new career direction entails.

My Current Admin Skills	*Why a Plus in NCD*
1. _____	_____
	_____
2. _____	_____
	_____
3. _____	_____
	_____
4. _____	_____
	_____
5. _____	_____
	_____
6. _____	_____
	_____

7. _____   _____
   _____

8. _____   _____
   _____

9. _____   _____
   _____

10. _____   _____
    _____

Let's return now to Barbara's days at the Kennedy School.

After wriggling out of that uncomfortable encounter with the professor, Barbara began paying regular visits to HR. Initially, these visits only kept that department aware that she was looking for something else, that she wanted to transfer to another department. Time and time again, she was told, "Nothing right now, Barbara, but we'll let you know."

But Barbara kept coming back. Over time, she built solid relationships with the HR staff, who got to know her personally as well as understand the exact situation she was looking for. This all paid off when one day a call came in to HR from one of the school's top deans. "Know any good administrators who could work in my office?" he asked. The HR assistant director who answered the phone thought of someone immediately. "We sure do," she said. Within a day or so, Barbara got the job!

See how it works? It's all about advertising, keeping your name in people's heads. When people need someone like you, you want to be the first person they think of. It's no secret, after all, why Burger King, McDonald's, and Wendy's all vie for your attention each evening starting around eight o'clock. They want to be the number-one fast food joint you rush off to when those late-night hunger pangs kick in. They know you've heard their names before, but they don't want you to forget them now. They

work hard at building a relationship with you—every night—
and with everyone you know.

Cut to Barbara again, now nestled in the gorgeous Colorado
Rockies.

This time our career heroine, jobless though focused, targeted advertising as her next career direction. Having just completed her
master's in mass communication, she'd been looking hard for any
kind of advertising position at all in the admittedly limited marketplace of Boulder.

Hoping to get a jump on the competition any way she could,
she began dropping by the office of the *Boulder Daily Camera* newspaper to check out its want ads before they even hit the street. By
popping in day after day just before noon, she soon became friendly
with the *Camera*'s receptionist, Jean.

"What kind of work are you looking for?" Jean asked Barbara
one day.

Barbara explained that working in some aspect of advertising
was her dream.

About a week or two later, Barbara came by just a little past her
usual time. Jean, very excited, waved her in. "I was wondering when
you'd get here," she cried. "There's something I've got to tell you."
The *Camera* itself, she said, would soon be looking for someone to
start as an account executive trainee in its advertising department.
No one else knew about this position yet, since it hadn't been advertised.

"And," Jean explained, "it won't be advertised if we find someone to fill it first."

Jean then introduced Barbara to the advertising manager, who
took her around to meet the rest of the staff. Before the week was
out, Barbara landed her first official job in advertising! Her career
ally, Jean, with whom she'd been having daily, off-the-cuff career
conversations, had come through for her, hook, line, and sinker.

Visiting Other Departments

Back to Marisa now. She'd made it a point to get to know someone in a department she was interested in, then followed up
with a visit there. She saw Merle's operation for herself and fur-

ther identified that she indeed wanted to work there. Remember that sometimes things in life fail to live up to our prior images, and work is certainly no exception. So Marisa needed to physically experience her potential new workplace in order to proceed to the next step of actually applying for a job.

Of course, Marisa had it easy, right? Since Merle had invited her, she didn't even have to raise the issue. But that's a typical scenario: Once you build an enjoyable career relationship with someone, they will want to help you in any way they can. They'll often surprise you by telling you about job openings, inviting you to visit their department (or company), introducing you to all the right people. Merle offered all of these and more.

It can get even better than that. We tried an experiment once during a career workshop in which we sent everyone out after lunch to do career conversations with strangers. Not just any strangers, however, but specifically with strangers who worked in positions of authority at companies our workshop participants knew they did not want to work for.

"Choose companies that do things that you don't care about," we instructed them. "And don't call ahead for appointments. Just drop in unexpectedly and ask to speak with a manager or someone else in authority. Then have a career conversation with them for around fifteen or twenty minutes about the work they do."

You can imagine the pessimism and shaking of heads in the room. As people left, few believed they would ever get an interview without an appointment. Even fewer imagined anything instructive could come of this assignment. "Why would I want to talk at length to someone doing work I don't care about?" they wanted to know.

Three hours later, everyone returned, chattering, excited, bushy-tailed. Before we could get out our official "How'd it go?" they began telling their stories.

"I got right in and spent an hour with a CEO," John said.

"I was treated to a tour of a company's entire facility," Elizabeth said.

"I met everyone who worked for this company," Kathleen said.

Said Alicia: "I got offered a job!"

Everyone turned toward Alicia. For a moment the room got quiet. We could see looks of shock on the faces of most of the others.

Suddenly a half-dozen new hands went up. "I got offered a job too," someone said. "Me too," said another. "Me too." "And me."

Tallying the results of this experiment, we found that of forty-eight workshop participants, forty had managed to get their impromptu meetings with persons of authority, and six of these had been offered—gasp!—jobs!

Had they asked for these jobs? Had they feigned interest in working for the companies they were visiting? Had they announced that they were job hunting? Had they handed over resumés, turned their career conversations into interviews?

All answers to these questions were no. They'd followed our instructions to the letter, letting the dynamics of human interaction take over. By simply presenting themselves in a non-threatening way, showing themselves to be curious and enthusiastic individuals, and taking a serious interest in the companies they were visiting, they had enabled their "hosts" to make judgments about them for themselves.

Why would this happen? Well, if there was a job opening at the moment, or a need to be filled, or a problem that hadn't yet been solved, these managers may have been waiting, perhaps subconsciously, for "the right person" to walk through their doors and save the day. Though these "right persons" had expressed no direct interest in working for the company, the managers could plainly see their potential. You could almost hear the following wheels turning in their heads:

"Hmmm, I have a hunch. I don't know much about this lady, but she seems to have a lot on the ball. Maybe she could handle this Allentown account for me. I wonder if she'd be interested in working here? I guess it wouldn't hurt to ask."

In your efforts, then, to explore opportunities that might be all around you, begin arranging meetings with people in their offices or making dates for what we call "opportunities luncheons" (or coffees or breakfasts) in the company cafeteria or at a nearby cafe or lunch spot. Explain to those you approach that you're curious about the work they do because you're conducting a "career educational campaign" for yourself. For that reason, you'd like to sit down sometime and talk about their work, their departments, their coworkers—anything that would familiarize you with a career area that intrigues you.

Don't worry at first about *who* you meet with. You could meet at first with an admin if you like to get yourself warmed up. Visiting departments gets you naturally in touch with decision-makers, technicians, salespeople, administrators. It lets you see firsthand how other departments run, and this tells you something about your next step: "Do I want to learn more?" "Am I still intrigued?" "Have I seen or met anyone in this initial surveillance whom I'd like to talk to again?"

Don't be afraid to pitch your "career education" idea to anybody and everybody. Sometimes we get intimidated by people in "high" positions or who seem so involved in what they're doing that they'd never offer us the time of day. But you'd be surprised! Remember, about 80 percent of our clients came back from successful meetings and six got offered jobs! When you strip away their facades people are just that: people! You'll be amazed at how approachable such "unapproachables" can really be.

Note of advice: When suggesting an "opportunity lunch" (or coffee or breakfast), always offer to buy. You may get waved off on this, but make a lunge for the check anyway. "Oh, it's OK, I really want to," you say. "When we get together again, we'll go to a really expensive place and then I'll let *you* pay." Ha-ha. Good one. Remember, the goodwill you'll create by asking for this meeting and then showing how much you appreciate it will go a long way toward solidifying your new relationship. If you make someone feel you've taken advantage of them, however, all your efforts will go right down the tubes.

"But, hey, Barbara and Ken, this is bound to get expensive!" Don't be too sure. That all depends on how you handle it, and also how you look at it. You can, for example, meet lots of folks for coffee at their offices where the java is free. Sometimes those you meet will in fact insist on at least paying for their share, if not the whole thing. One of our admin clients once had a manager say to her, "Listen, I'll let you pick up the check next time—after your promotion!"

You've also got to consider any expense you incur as an investment. When you think about a potential raise in income of, say, $2,000 to $5,000 initially and of who knows how much in the long run, your return on investment for lunches and coffees starts looking pretty good. This isn't money washing down the drain, after all; it's your travel and entertainment budget. Starting now, my friend, you're going places.

Stepping Out

Speaking of spending money, we have another gem of a suggestion for you. For a nominal fee here and there, you can garner all the career conversations you could ever want. In most cases you won't have to ask people, approach people, or persuade anyone. Your new career allies will walk right over to you.

What the heck are we talking about? Why, professional organizations and special events, silly.

Which nonprofit association represents the new career of your choice? Thinking of going into sales? There's undoubtedly a chapter of the Sales and Marketing Executives of America nearby. Contemplating academia? How about checking in on the local branch of the National Teachers Association? Got your heart set on a career as a bank loan officer? Go attend the monthly meeting of the American Bankers Association somewhere in your area.

There's a trade group for every endeavor, and you could do worse than participate in those that are relevant to your interests. For a fee of ten, twenty, maybe thirty dollars, you can walk into a hotel function room and immediately strike up a conversation with whoever is standing over by the hors d'oeuvres. You'll learn about trends in the industry, how particular individuals view their professions, who the major companies are in the area, who among these companies are currently hiring, how people got started in this business—the whole ball of wax!

Effortlessly, you'll encounter career conversations breaking out all over the joint, and you'll also get an educational program with an expert in the field speaking on a topic you'll find fascinating. You may even get a hot meal to boot. Wowee-zowee! Who could ask for anything more?

You'll also want to check out conferences and trade shows. There are always special events of this type going on, frequently sponsored by your local professional organization. Join one of these organizations, and you'll receive mailings that will alert you to such events. Again, investing in a conference, trade show, or other special event can only do you good. It educates you professionally, it puts you in touch with the movers and shakers of the field, and it feeds your ears with opportunities. It also gives you the chance to socialize and have a bit of fun as you move your professional life along.

Bonus: If you really want to get some mileage out of professional organizations, conferences, and special events, get involved "behind the scenes." Are you curious about the training and development field? Join your local chapter of the American Society of Training and Development and volunteer for committee work. Maybe you'll work on the chapter newsletter, the program committee, the membership committee—whatever you'd most enjoy. That way you'll build new career relationships *really* fast, as well as become quickly knowledgeable and well known in the field.

And, if you're trying to stay within a budget, help out with programming or conference planning. That way you'll get to go to many events free of charge as a volunteer staffer. You'll also get to know intimately some of the top people in the field as you rub shoulders with them "backstage."

Making Your Boss Your Mentor

You may recall that at the beginning of this book we gave you three scenarios of common kinds of admin experiences and asked if any of them rang true. The scenario that might have seemed most out of place was the third, in which our admin heroine (Barbara, remember?) found herself in an interview with a manager who said, "Anything I can do to help you professionally, just ask. I see this as a partnership, a two-way street."

While such attitudes on the part of admins' supervisors are not unheard of, for many admins they seem about as close to home as the far side of the moon. In other words, practically speaking, they don't exist.

So let's talk about how to *make* them exist. It could be, for example, that your boss has already given you signals that he's more than willing to mentor you, but you haven't picked up on them. Or it could be that, given the right coaching (by you), he could get that way. Whatever the case, too many admins assume their bosses have no interest in helping them along. Frequently nothing could be farther from the truth.

Paul Falcone, author of *The Complete Job-Finding Guide for Secretaries and Administrative Support Staff*, says, "Without your boss' support, you'll have to proceed quietly and that's tough. Other managers probably won't even want to talk to you if they know your boss doesn't approve. But you can probably make your boss your mentor, which is the best scenario."

How does one elicit mentorship from one's boss? Try these questions on for size:

1. Do you currently enjoy open, free communication with your boss? Can you talk to him, offer ideas, tell him when you're feeling overworked, confused? Does he give you time off when you need it?
2. Does your boss ever confide his feelings in you or ask you for favors? Does he offer to do favors for you? Does he ask you frequently how you are doing?
3. Does your boss offer to send you to training programs and outside seminars and conferences? Does he see you as a resource to be developed? Does he ever bring in outside consultants to train his staff (including you) and to help everyone grow professionally?
4. Is he patient with your mistakes? Does he recognize that learning takes time? Does he pitch in and help you whenever "crunch" time rolls around?

After reading these questions, what's your general reaction? Your boss doesn't have to do or feel *all* of these things. What we're talking about here is his potential.

Have you ever actually asked your boss to mentor you? Have you asked him if he'll pay for any professional trainings you might be interested in? Have you asked if you could attend trainings that are not strictly admin-related, such as an accounting seminar, an engineering conference, a sales training program—something you're exploring and would like to learn more about?

Remember, in today's "post-job" society you've got to do all the initiating yourself. More people are willing to help you than you know, but you've got to pick up the ball and explain to them how. Your boss is no exception.

If you're unsure about your boss-as-mentor, first test the waters. Falcone advises that you start by seeking reimbursement and/or time off for a training program or workshop, especially a "non–admin" one. Find something that interests you, then propose the idea to your boss. If he says yes, you'll know you're on to something. Your next step might be to strike up a conversation about career advancement in general—that is, what are his feelings about how people should try to get ahead in these difficult times? See what he says. If all this feels positive, go one step further: Ask him about helping you out. He may very well say yes.

"But, hey, Ken and Barbara, what if my boss says no to a training reimbursement and gives every indication that he thinks career advancement is for him and his buddies and nobody else?" Well, then, ladies and gentlemen, you've got, as we say in the business, "a problem"! Not an insurmountable one, mind you, but a problem all the same.

What to Do When Your Boss *Won't* Mentor You

Obviously, when your boss won't be your mentor, you have two choices: (1) Find someone else, or (2) find two or more "someone elses."

Is there a formal mentoring system in your company? If not, could you start one? You do have to be a little cautious here because you don't want a nonsupportive boss to see you spending too much of your time thinking about moving on and not enough on your work for him. But if you keep up with the day's workload in a cheery and energetic fashion, there shouldn't be trouble. With a formal system in place, you'll be part of an official structure, so who could blame you for your participation?

On the other hand, if there's no formal structure and you

can't start one, you'd best go about enlisting the aid of a mentor on the q.t. Not that you need to keep the whole thing top secret; just don't broadcast it. Do what you have to do, attend to your official responsibilities, and then, whenever possible, attend to your career responsibilities as well.

Find Someone Else

Finding anything will usually revolve around our number-one career advancement technique, the career conversation.

How can you use career conversations to find the proper mentor? Tut, tut, nothing to it: Just ask around.

You'll begin by asking people for nominations "in confidence." The very process of asking folks for help will enroll them in your career advancement campaign. It'll involve many to such an extent that *they'll* become impromptu mentors for you right there on the spot. An "instant mentor" system—we love it!

Put together a few criteria when you begin your solicitations. You'll want to find a mentor who's really right for you, after all. What kind of person do you want to find? There are some objective standards we can recommend, but after all is said and done you've got to tailor your search for the "perfect match" for *you*. Choose criteria based on the kind of pesonality you prefer and experience you admire. Much of it, of course, will be a gut reaction: "Do I like this person?" "Do I feel confident about her commitment to me?" "Do I respect his ideas?"

Along with your personal criteria for choosing the right mentor, here are other criteria to keep in mind:

1. Pick someone who's *positive*. You want a mentor who will keep your spirits up during the downs as well as during the ups.
2. Pick someone who's been *through the mill*. Success usually delivers less personal growth than failure. Find a mentor who understands failure as part of the mix and thus can counsel you whenever it rears its all-too-familiar plug-ugly head.
3. Pick someone who understands that *credentials aren't everything*, especially these days. Your mentor should be

aware that change is here to stay. Upgrading our value by continual reeducation will breed more success than leaning on past educational triumphs and training. All is in flux.
4. Pick someone who *knows a lot of people.* One can't have too many career conversations or career allies; it's just not possible. Much of your advancement success will rest on others getting to know you, and you them. Find a mentor who understands that.

Set down on the following lines *your* criteria for a mentor who's right for you. Jot down any ideas that come to mind. What can you add to our list of "objective" criteria?

_____

_____

_____

_____

_____

Appoint a Board of Mentors

Remember how we suggested finding "two or more somebody elses" to serve as your mentor(s)? Well, here's what we mean: Companies set up boards of directors to advise them on their business strategies, correct? Such board members are frequently selected with the same criteria you'll have in mind for your mentor. So why not set up a board of directors for yourself? Maybe we should call it your board of mentors?

Certainly, two (or more) heads can be better than one and more individuals invested in genuinely assisting you in your career advancement campaign are likely to result in a multiplicity of eyes and ears out there in the streets (or in the suites) for you.

So scout around, if you're inclined, for more than one mentor. Maybe you'll set up a monthly meeting in which everyone gets a couple of big, fat, juicy slices of deep-dish pizza (your treat, of course) and a chance to do some career advancement interaction of their own (with other "board" members). You'll be surprised how much fun a technique like this one can bring to the overall process.

Making Your Presence Known

When people get to know us and like us, they will do their best to help, no matter what our backgrounds. That doesn't mean they will sponsor us for a job we're not qualified for, or a job that they doubt we can do, but it does mean that they'll sponsor us when we do seem right for a job. So a next order of business when seeking to extricate yourself from the pink-collar ghetto is to get qualified in the new career direction of your choice.

You'll do this by returning to school, or enrolling in a relevant training program, or learning to explain how your current skill set is transferable, or becoming an apprentice or assistant to an established expert.

As usual, you'll need to continue to build your career relationships. You can do this in ways we've been describing, but you can supplement it through any number of techniques that make you more visible. That's a neat trick for the admin because even though one would think an admin is more visible than most—she's often, for example, the first voice heard or face seen when someone calls upon a decision-maker—admins, as we know, are too easily dismissed as flunkies and gatekeepers and thus not seen for their value or their potential.

So make yourself more visible via one or more of the following techniques:

- *Public speaking.* Almost everybody hates to do it, and even some celebrities (Carly Simon and Barbra Streisand, just to mention two) hate to get up in front of others so much that they stay off stages and platforms for years.

Yet those of us who do do it stand out. There's an instant credibility that comes with getting up before others, even when we're obviously nervous or inexperienced. "She's got guts to get up there," many in the audience will say to themselves. And that's how you want people to feel about you—that you're willing to do what it takes, no matter what.

Where can you "public speak," especially if you're just getting started? First, you can practice by raising your hand at meetings and sharing your thoughts whenever you get a chance. That'll also help get you more comfortable.

You can volunteer to introduce other speakers at meetings, luncheons, or other events, or to moderate or take part in panel discussions. This way you'll get practice getting up there in front of a sea of strange faces without having to stay up there too long. Just thirty seconds here and there could build your confidence dramatically.

To get really into the swing of public speaking, join a Toastmasters' Club at your local library and volunteer to speak at meetings and conferences sponsored by your relevant professional organization, church group, civic association. There are plenty of opportunities around. Stand up, speak up, and you'll be seen and heard by everyone.

▪ *Task forces and committees.* Is there a quality-control committee, a marketing-ideas committee, a customer-relations committee—anything that you as an employee can get involved in with others in your company? If there is, then get on it! You'll substantially raise your visibility by interacting with others over substantive issues and helping make hard decisions and recommendations. Just one or two tours of duty and you might even be elected the committee chair. That'll *really* raise your credibility level!

And remember, this same technique works when you're looking to gain visibility outside your company or if you're unemployed and looking for a new position. Join committees within your relevant professional organization or task forces set up to study a governmental problem. Vie for positions on a board of directors that governs a private company or a nonprofit agency. Once again, no one on a committee or observing its work will in any way view you as "just an admin."

▪ *Company newsletter.* Say, remember when you were editor of your high school yearbook? Or a reporter for the school newspaper? Well, guess what—you can do any or all of that all over again! And right here within the comfort of your current company!

The company newsletter (or annual report or closed-circuit TV system) frequently gets overlooked as a magnificent vehicle for visibility. Think about it: You can write for it, edit it, take photos for it, get written about in it, get your photo taken for it, get an announcement about you printed in it. Just take the view that you *love* publicity any way you can get it!

Make sure, of course, that any publicity you do get advances your professional goals and stature. For example, if you want to transition to management, write an article about new management techniques, do a book review of a new management best-seller, or get yourself interviewed about management techniques used by you in your own work.

Any "don'ts" you'll want to beware of? Sure: anything that reinforces your image as an admin. Therefore, no recipes, no sewing tips, no essays entitled "Why I Love My Boss" (please!), no photos of you typing or filing or taking shorthand. Your purpose is to drag yourself out of that pink-collar ghetto, remember? Don't affix lead weights to your ankles as you try to do so.

Whom Can I Approach?

In a notebook you've purchased just for this purpose, start listing everyone you can think of who might qualify as a career ally. List name, address, phone number, and relevant professional and personal details.

Next, start categorizing according to priority. Who's an *A* whom you want to approach first, who's a *B*, who's a *C*? Some you might want to send a letter to first; others you'll just pick up the phone and call. Leave space to mark down what happens as you begin making contact. Who accepted your calls? Who returned your calls? Who agreed to meet with you? Who's been great? Who's a dud?

If you have access to a computer, enter all this data on a special file. Keeping accurate and complete records helps you know whom to call to answer your questions about particular departments, companies, hiring managers. That's how the successful, high-achievement professionals go about this.

And you're rapidly becoming one of those.

"You've Got to Put New Ideas Out There"

A "Q and A" with Paul Falcone

Author of *The Complete Job-Finding Guide for Secretaries and Administrative Support Staff,* Paul Falcone is a human resources manager for Aames Financial Corporation in Los Angeles. He is former director of training and contingency recruiting with The London Agency, a placement firm specializing in administrative support recruitment. Paul holds a master's degree from UCLA and three certifications in human resources management, and he gives motivational speeches throughout the United States.

Ken Lizotte: Paul, what holds many admins back from advancing their careers?

Paul Falcone: Many admins feel trapped because they try to go from A to Z, and it can't be done. You've got to go to B first, but people don't always recognize that.

For example, a lot of admins think about going into management but fail to observe that you've got to have a certain background to go into any field, and in management that's often sales and marketing. So first you want to go to B—sales and marketing. After you've gotten sufficient experience there, you'll be qualified to move on.

K.L.: What else holds them back?

P.F.: Being afraid to take a risk. You can have a "factory mentality," where you're always worried about security and you just follow orders, or you can have an "entrepreneurial mentality," which is the way of the future. To open up more responsibilities, you've got to get management recognition, and that means putting yourself on the line. You've got to make your performance truly affect the bottom line.

K.L.: How can admins do that?

P.F.: Show that you can cut costs and save your company time. You've got to put new ideas out there, take a chance. You might get slapped on the wrist for even trying, but if you don't try you won't stand a chance at being noticed.

This isn't always easy in a larger company, by the way.

In larger companies, everybody's a specialist, everything's organized around functions. In a smaller company, though, there's often more room for self-expression and for impacting the firm. So if your advancement strategies aren't working at a large company that you work for, think about moving to a company that's small.

K.L.: How can you enlist your boss in your efforts to advance?

P.F.: It all depends on your relationship with your boss. My assumption is that you and your boss enjoy open communication. If so, make your boss your mentor. Ask for what you need: information about other departments or careers, introductions to contacts, reimbursement for trainings and workshops.

K.L.: What if you don't get it?

P.F.: If you can't make your boss your mentor, you may have to move on. It's really tough to advance in a company if your boss is not supportive. No one else within the company will want to hire you for fear of alienating your present boss.

K.L.: How can your company's customers help you advance?

P.F.: You may find yourself interested in working for someone who does business with your employer. If so, go to them discreetly and say, "I've done everything here I can, and it seems that the option doesn't exist for me to advance much further. If something surfaces in your company, I'd love to be considered."

K.L.: What do *you* look for when you're hiring someone? Would you ever hire someone with only admin positions on her resumé?

P.F.: We hire admins to do "postadmin" jobs all the time! I look for people who seem to have a track record for reinventing their jobs in light of a company's changing needs. People who have a global perspective will find ways to add value to their company; they can see how they fit into the overall unit. If you're the kind of person who likes to figure out better ways to do a process, you'll show yourself to be more than "just" an admin. Remember, it's the "entrepreneurial" mentality everyone's looking for. If you can show people that, you'll go places.

FROM THE ADMIN FILES

Name of ex-admin: Mary Miller

Currently: Administrator of marketing and enrollment for four health insurance plans at Massachusetts Institute of Technology, directing efforts to enroll employees and students in relevant health-care programs.

How change was made: "An ad in the newspaper caught my eye. I knew the department because I had worked at MIT previously. In the office I had worked in before, we had been involved in scrutinizing all other departments, including this one. Ultimately, the executive director who hired me had been impressed by the job I was doing at my previous position. So I had 'auditioned' for the job without even knowing it."

Admin skills used today: Organizing, planning, scheduling, setting up agendas

Best advice to admins: "Get visible! I used to walk into personnel offices to interview for admin positions and the first thing they'd do is put me down in front of a typewriter to check my speed. It was devastating to my self-esteem! It seemed like the only thing they figured I could do.

"Yet I knew myself better. I knew I could bring people together, sell, market, gain people's trust quickly and easily. I just needed to be given a chance. The way I got it was that someone had observed me doing all that because I had gotten visible by hosting high-level meetings. So when the day came that I walked into her office to interview for the position I hold now, she knew me as more than just another admin."

7

Career Treasure Chest

Rachel is beginning to get depressed. She's been an executive admin for the VP of product development at a major electronics firm for about twelve years, and she is desperately overdue for a change. But everywhere she sends her resumé, the same message comes back: "We'll keep your resumé on file. Sorry, no openings at the moment."

In one way each rejection relieves her. She doesn't want to continue as an executive admin for anybody anyway. She only applies for these positions because she doesn't know what else to do. "What else am I qualified for?" she keeps asking herself.

But her depression really begins setting in as the volume of rejection letters piles up. "Nobody wants you," they seem to scream at her. "Stay where you are!"

Unfortunately, this very unpretty picture plays itself out each and every day in the lives of hundreds of thousands of otherwise very competent, very astute professionals. Its assumptions lie in outmoded ideas about how one looks for work as well as a personal dearth of self-confidence about one's chances for success in a new field. Sadly, most of us accept these outmoded assumptions as the "only way" or the obvious, natural strategy. We then justify this thinking by exclaiming: "I don't know any other way to do it!" And that's really interesting to us because as we've counseled hundreds and hundreds of career explorers over the years, we've heard the same thing from many professionals who ought to know better. We're thinking here of top sales pros, of marketing and advertising geniuses, and of research experts. Come to think of it, we've heard it from job-hunting career counselors too!

All of these pros incorporate many of the principles we espouse for carrying out a creative career advancement plan in their regular professional lives, but even they fall back on the traditional avenues of job search once they are out on their own: Write out your resumé, check the want ads in the Sunday paper, mail out your resumés on Monday—then wait!

Assumptions That Need to Be Challenged

1. We can apply only for work we've done before.
2. We must base most of our advancement plan on want ads.
3. The smart thing is to dutifully mail out resumés Monday morning, then passively wait for a reply.
4. Job hunting, by definition, is a lonely endeavor.
5. Lots of rejection letters mean that nobody wants you.

Given these ways of going about the process, it's no wonder Rachel's spirits began to sink.

Upending Rachel's Assumptions

We don't really know where or when we all picked up the kinds of signals that got us into this mess, but we do know this: If you're going to be effective in advancing your career, outmoded job-search thinking has got to go! Rachel's no different from the rest of us. She fell smack into the same trap that keeps most folks from scrambling back up onto solid ground and staying on course toward their dreams. We could sum up the problem with two insidious little words: *isolation* and *passivity*.

Rachel let herself buy the notion of her limited value to the marketplace. But we've seen how it's possible to extend your value in the marketplace and transform it into something new, something exciting, refreshing, conducive to growth. In the same way, we need to rethink tools, resources, job-search techniques, and other "treasures" in our career treasure chests so they'll be more effective in advancing our dreams.

One way that might aid us in this world would be to challenge all of Rachel's assumptions.

Rachel's Assumption 1:   You can apply only for work you've done before.

Flip Side: Embrace work you want.

As you gather together your board of mentors, meet with your career allies, and visit coworkers in other departments, you'll want to be sure you communicate what you most want them to hear. That means drawing conclusions from the research and career conversations you've been conducting thus far. Sit yourself down now (oh, you're already sitting, aren't you?) and contemplate the following "career questions." Insert any answers you've come up with on the lines provided beneath each question:

1. *Of all the career options you've been exploring, which ones most motivate and excite you? List at least one, no more than three.*

_____

_____

_____

2. *What kinds of people would you most like to work with? Describe in detail the work atmosphere you'd most like to find.*

_____

_____

_____

3. *Where would you like your new situation to be located? How far from your home, in what direction? How much travel would you like to be doing?*

_____

_____

_____

4. *What kind of compensation are you looking for? Include not only your income goals but benefits, vacation time, investment options, health plan.*

_____

_____

_____

5. *Where would you like to be in the future? Describe how you see your next position fitting into your career plans five years from now.*

_____

_____

_____

Career Visioning

Now take your answers and compose your "career vision." In the frame on the next page, illustrate with colored markers or crayons exactly the kind of career move you want to make. Be sure to include *all* details listed above.

Once you've finished your drawing, complete this phrase, using the space provided below:

My career vision consists of:

_____

_____

_____

_____

_____

Congratulations! You are well on your way now to clarifying what you want. Of course you will probably need to continue career conversations to flesh out many of these details or to refine them and weight how realistic your career idea is. But no matter: As long as you keep thinking and writing down new

My Career Vision

ideas and researching details, your career vision will become more and more real and attainable.

What if you listed more than one career option? Say you like two or three equally and you're beside yourself trying to figure out which one to really go after. Well, how's this for a wild idea: Choose them all!

Many professionals today have caught on to a trick businesses have been hip to for years. It's called diversification. In simple terms, you commit yourself to a professional life that integrates two or more career areas at once. In addition to allowing you to enjoy your overall work life more, diversifying provides a level of security that relying on only one source of income cannot.

Graduates of our programs who have gone this route include a former admin who now operates a desktop publishing business during the day and offers massage on nights and weekends, an ex-admin who now teaches Spanish at a community college while also running a dance studio, an ex-secretary who teaches English-as-a-second-language two days a week and works in a college admissions office the other three.

If, however, this "career mosaic" approach doesn't ring true for you, just keep exploring, researching, career conversing. At some point, you'll find yourself spending most of your energy on one or the other of your career directions. That may spell out your answer.

Rachel's Assumption 2:	Base your career advancement campaign on want ads.
Flip Side:	Use want ads as clues.

You've heard it before, we're sure: Classified help-wanted ads represent only the tiniest percentage of the job market. Plus they're the ultimate in fostering isolation and passivity. Think about it: You know little about the job, little or nothing about the employer, nothing at all about who will interview you, little about compensation, working conditions, and the job's future.

Next, you're supposed to follow orders in the want ad to a T: Mail in your resumé (no phone calls please), including your "salary requirements" and references from everybody you've ever met. What? Shouldn't you crate your mother and dog off to them too?

If you're looking for work *outside* your company, carry on exactly as we've advised you so far regarding methods for seeking a change *inside* your company—that is, build relationships, conduct career conversations, create visibility. High-energy, people-oriented day-to-day activities should absorb at least 80 percent of your efforts.

What do you do with the other 20 percent? Answer ads, if you like, but also use them as clues. Understand that ads are like icebergs: You can easily see the very tip, but there's a lot more where that came from beneath the surface.

Say that you're interested in working in customer service. You see a couple of ads for customer service. Make a note of the kind of company that's doing the advertising.

Then on Monday, after you've mailed out your resumé to these ads, get on the phone and call other companies of the same stripe who might be in the market for a good customer service rep.

Don't call human resources, though; call the customer service department directly. Strike up a friendly career chat with one of the reps and let her direct you to her manager. If there's a job available and you're prepared to present yourself for it, go to it. If you're still researching customer service work, however, ask to come in for a career conversation or an opportunity lunch. The key, as we've been saying, is to build relationships.

Ads, then, offer clues that other work is out there. Gather whatever data such ads offer, then file them in your memory bank. If you follow clues to companies that aren't advertising, you might meet decision-makers who've been waiting, without knowing it, to meet you.

Rachel's Assumption 3:   Mail out resumés and wait passively
                         for a reply.
Flip Side: Never use a resumé.

This one's a typo, right? This has got to be a mistake. Or maybe we're joking. Actually, we mean what we say. If possible, *never* use a resumé. In your situation, it will rarely help.

"But Ken and Barbara," all of you are wailing, "how can I not have a resumé? I've *got* to have a resumé; everybody's got to have a resumé. What're ya talking about, Ken and Barbara, no resumé?"

We hear you. We hear you. Yes, you ought to *have* a resumé. We're just telling you never to *use* it! Got that? You see, many of our more successful clients have made their career switches in just this way. In fact, many of the most successful people we've ever met gave up using resumés long ago. That's because the way they handle their career activities—again, through building career relationships, ongoing career conversations, and participation in professional organizations—makes a resumé unnecessary.

Resumés generally are requested by people who aren't sold on you yet. Your resumé then acts as a buffer, a means of further scrutiny, or a way to get off the hook (or off the phone). "Well, send me your resumé and we'll talk again later." Yeah, right!

After sending your resumé, you'll usually become a dead issue—conversation over, resumé filed, on to the next candidate (or project). If your resumé does get a lengthy look-see, you'll probably be judged as not qualified for the position you're applying for.

And it's no secret why: Your resumé trumpets, in great detail, the you who has spent years as an admin. Unless you've put your resumé together very cleverly and creatively, it won't advertise your potential, your enthusiasm, your ability to learn new things, or your intense motivation to grow. Rather than serve up an accurate picture of who you are and who you can be, it depicts only one very limited side of you—your experience as an admin.

Still and all—sigh!—there will be times when you really ought to have one. Even if you do everything we say in this book, such as building a vast empire of career relationships, here and there you may be asked for a resumé in good faith.

Example: "I'd really like to get you into my department, Claire, but the company does require that I file your resumé. Welcome to my staff! Just let me have your resumé as a formality and we'll be in business."

At this point, you'll want to hand over a resumé that speaks exactly to the reasons you're being hired, those characteristics you've sold your new boss on—your talents, relevant skills, enthusiasm, potential. You want your new employers to say, "Yes-sir, here we have it: We hired the right gal!"

Another reason to have a resumé, though—and in some ways perhaps your best reason—might be as an exercise to clar-ify further your new value in the marketplace. You can't ask yourself too often what you want, and likewise you can never get too clear about what you might offer to a new employer. Revising your resumé can substantially upgrade your under-standing of your "work self."

Now what kind of a resumé would be right for you? How can you paint yourself as something other than an admin when that's all you've ever been? Well, since most of us have been schooled in resumé-writing to put down everything we've done in our work lives starting from our present job and then listing all the others backward chronologically, we're bound to be con-fused. We've grown up thinking that's the only way.

But another style of resumé-writing focuses on talents, abili-ties, and achievements, and that's the one that works best for anyone making a move in a new career direction. Many career advisers call this a functional-style resumé, but we personally find that term clinical and drab.

Example: "Tell me, chum, just what 'functions' do you per-form on your present job?"

God, are we talking about machinery here or human be-ings?

Let's just call this a success-style resumé and leave it at that. That should keep us thinking positively.

Success-Style Resumé Close-Up

So let's get started! Go back now through the exercises in previous chapters and take a fresh look at your talents, skills, and achievements. How many of these are relevant to the excit-ing new career direction you've come up with so far? If you've conducted plenty of career conversations and done lots of read-ing, you'll have some answers.

Focus on only one career direction per resumé. If you're thinking about going for two or more, you've got to fashion a resumé to serve each. Computers, of course, now make it possible to do this, as well as to tailor resumés to particular jobs, companies, or departments. Your career conversations will help you understand particular priorities and values inherent in each situation. You then incorporate whatever information about you seems relevant, emphasizing the most relevant by placing it higher on the page. You can also drop irrelevant information so that it doesn't get in the way.

Take a gander at this sample we've drawn up for you in Figure 7-1.

What kind of work do you suppose Elizabeth (Liza) is seeking? What work do you suppose she's best qualified for? Would you be likely to surmise from this resumé that Liza has spent her entire career as an admin?

Yet there's nothing false about the way Liza has structured this description of her professional history and abilities. She's merely made it relevant to the work she's seeking. Her objective is to help potential employers see clearly how she can fit in.

The old school (Rachel's school) heaps all the onus for figuring out how you might fit in on someone else—a potential boss, manager, employer, human resources representative. Yet those folks can know only what you tell them about you. They can't know what new things you're capable of unless you make a case for it. Thus rather than wait for a job interview to make this case (as Rachel would do), you get right down to the business of selling yourself in this resumé.

Which only makes sense, of course, because if you don't sell yourself from the get-go, how are you going to land that job interview in the first place?

Putting Your Success-Style Resumé Together

To compose your own success-style resumé, first loosen yourself up: wriggle your fingers and toes, roll your neck around a few times, shrug your shoulders up and down. People often get very tense about putting together their resumé. You don't have to. This document will liberate you. It'll be an expression of your dreams and of your Best Self. Really.

1. *List all talents, skills, and achievements you find to be relevant to your new career direction.* Make this list as long as you like—

Figure 7-1. Sample Success-Style Resumé

Elizabeth Doolittle
5 Hartford Street
Hereford, New Hampshire 02119
603-555-8761

Achievements
- Coordinated over 100 focus groups consisting of up to 500 clients each (Alfred Beverage Company)
- Processed more than 10,000 customer survey projects, including tabulation of 3,500 customer service questionnaires (Alfred Beverage Company, Pickering Institute)
- Participated actively in Customer Response Committee (Rex Corporation)
- Administered and supervised correspondence of approximately 5,000 letters with major clientele (all employers)

Skills
- Excellent client liaison skills
- Knowledge of marketing-oriented customer relations
- Excellent administrative skills and software expertise

Professional History
- Client Service Coordinator—Alfred Beverage Company, Salem, New Hampshire
- Client Service Assistant—Pickering Institute, Manchester, New Hampshire
- Customer Traffic Manager—Rex Corporation, Londonderry, New Hampshire

Education
- Customer Service Skills Certificate—American Management Association seminar
- Direct Marketing Skills Course—Hookset Junior College
- Communication Skills for Women—Manchester (NH) Adult Education Center
- Business Administration Associates Degree—Katherine Gibbs School, Boston—was graduated with honors

Personal Interests
- Treasurer, local chapter, Customer Service Association of America
- Greeter, Community Church of Hereford (NH)
- Author of *Guidelines for Good Member Relations,* a handbook for the Hereford, New Hampshire, YWCA

you can cut it down later. Do this on a computer if at all possible because you'll then be able to revise and play around with your list easily. If you don't have access to a computer, use as many sheets of paper as you need.

2. *List every place you've worked in your professional life.* (Again, if you're not using a computer, fill up a separate sheet of paper.) Put down a title for yourself first, then the name of your employer (or department) underneath. If possible, make sure the job title sounds as if it's connected to the kind of work you want to do next. Try to think of something that describes your work in this position accurately but slants it in your new career direction. Don't just write "admin, admin, admin" if you can help it.

You may need your present boss or past one to back you on your descriptive title. If he, she, or they won't do it, you'll have to make a judgment call. As long as you can make a case for the descriptive title you've put down, it'll probably be worth getting challenged about it. Obviously you don't want to just make stuff up. But you've got to find a way to sound like something other than "just an admin."

What's an example? Look back at Liza's resumé. In seeking a new career direction in customer service, she labeled herself a client liaison in her two previous jobs and a customer liaison in her first job. In fact, these positions had been listed officially as administrative assistant, secretary, and receptionist, in that order. But those are no more descriptive of what she really did at each job than her more creative titles. In fact, they were *less* descriptive.

So why not make her job in each situation sound directly relevant to customer service? We know she did a lot of customer service–type work; why shouldn't she get credit for it? What you're aiming for here is *more* accuracy rather than less.

"But, hey, Ken and Barbara, what about me? I want to go into the landscaping business. How the heck am I going to get around that? Admin work and landscaping are like night and day!"

Three-word answer: Use your imagination. Ask yourself what kind of work an admin does that landscapers also perform. Have you ever tended to the details and the overall aesthetics of your office environment? Have you ever brought flowers in to keep on your desk? Did you ever water the plants? Maybe you helped select the paintings on the walls? There's probably a lot an admin does that connects even to the landscaping business. Think about it. Maybe you weren't "just an admin," filing, typing letters, going for coffee. Maybe you might also have been called the company's "lobby aesthetics manager" or "officescape administrator" or "interior environmental coordinator."

In truth, we picked this one because it's a longer stretch than something like customer service. We wanted to show you that by using your imagination (and if at all possible the support of your current or previous boss), you can probably come up with something that both is accurate and portrays you in a non–admin light.

"But hey, Barbara and Ken, that's all well and good, but won't any potential employers know what I'm doing and chuck my resumé away?"

Some might, but most probably will not. Especially if you're relying on building career relationships to get you in the door rather than just mailing out resumés to ads. The worst that's likely to happen is they'll at least call you out of curiosity to better understand what your resumé means. But that's good because that's what you wanted—to be able to talk to somebody.

Once you've got them on the phone, you can explain that, yes, you did perform lots of conventional admin duties, but you also wanted them to know all about your landscaping-related activities as well. If you bubble over with enthusiasm for this line of work and get them excited about your knowledge, passion, and readiness to move in this direction, you're likely to at least get called in for an interview. Basically, you've told them exactly what they needed to know—that you're the sort of dynamic candidate for this landscaping gig they've been looking for.

3. *List your schooling* in the third section of your resumé, at the bottom of the page (and try to keep it to just one page). If you have a degree of any kind, put it down. If you've taken any *relevant* courses anywhere else, list those. Our admin/landscape

designer, for example, might list educational experiences such as "Flora and Fauna, An Overview" at the Freetown Arboretum or "Gardening for Fun and Profit" at the Freetown Adult Education Center. Anything in your experience that relates directly to your new career direction should go down here. Everything that's relevant builds your credibility. *Note:* If you have only a high school education and nothing else—no adult ed courses, no junior college certificates, no one-day workshops, nothing!—then leave this entire section out.

4. *Should you list dates?* That's a tough one. If you're building your career relationships, of course, this probably won't matter. Face-to-face, met with your fire and enthusiasm, most potential employers will tend to let the age question (whether "too old" or "too young") melt away.

If you're flying blind, however, sending your resumé out to employers unseen, you'll want to convey that you're stable and that you don't fly around from employer to employer at the drop of a hat. Yet some employees think five years at one company is too long while others think that's too few. So it's a crap shoot.

That's why we're going to suggest you leave dates out. Let potential employers you haven't met call you to discern your age, if that's what they care about, illegal as that may be. Again, once they call you, you've got them. You'll just turn on the ol' admin-on-the-way-up charm and win them over.

5. *Should you list personal interests?* If they're relevant, sure. Our admin/landscaper might list "rose garden, attending annual flower show, avid viewer of *The Flower Shop* TV program." Does this sound amateurish, vapid, silly? Maybe, but when you're making a major career change and your professional qualifications are limited, again you've got to pull out all the stops. To *not* mention these interests would be to imply they don't exist. The way we figure it, this kind of omission misleads readers of your resumé by implying you don't have near the enthusiasm, knowledge, or experience you really do. Put it in.

6. *How about job objective or summary of qualifications?* Nah, readers of your resumé will understand what you're looking for and why you're qualified for it if you've structured the contents properly. Just cut to the chase.

So what do we have here? A success-style resumé, perhaps? Just about. All you've got to do now is:

- Cut down your "achievements" and "skills" section to manageable size. Cull relevant items from that long list we asked you to make in step 1 on page 133. Fit "talents" into whichever section seems most appropriate, or combine with "skills"—i.e., "talents and skills."
- Make sure your achievements are not only relevant but quantifiable, that is, with numbers included if possible. (Liza's resumé does this well. Take a look at it.)
- Position what you deem to be the most impressive items on the top of your list.
- Add in headings.
- Print out the whole masterpiece on "resumé paper." (See your local printer for samples.)

Do all of these things and voilà!—ya got yourself one dang fancy resumé, pardner.

What About Cover Letters?

Many human resources directors tell us they consider cover letters more an annoyance than anything else. They brush right past them and on to the resume. That means your time may be better spent polishing the resumé itself than your opening epistle.

If you must write a cover letter, however, make it brief and to the point. Get through the niceties quickly and focus your second paragraph on what you most want your prospective employer to know about you. But don't make it a tome.

Rachel's Assumption 4:   Job-hunting is something you do alone.
Flip Side: Always bring others along.

If you haven't adopted what we call a "careermate" by now, then get on with it! Traditionally people think of career transitions as solitary endeavors. Yet it must be obvious to you by now that we hold a different view. Why else would we recommend career allies, building career relationships, mentors, and personal boards of mentors? There's no reason in the world you need take this walk alone. People are willing to walk with you.

What's a careermate? Basically, she's your teammate, your buddy, your career best friend. The relationship often works best when your careermate is currently engaged in a career transition too, or has recently made one, because then she'll understand what you're going through. But whatever her situation, she'll make a commitment to work with you and to help you keep going, and if she needs the same thing, you'll commit yourself to her as well.

Be careful, however, whom you choose. You need someone positive, creative, resourceful, and who cares about you. Ask yourself the following questions when considering careermate candidates:

- Is my potential careermate someone who has proved in the past to have my best interests at heart?
- Is my potential careermate someone who will push me when I need to be pushed?
- Does my potential careermate listen closely to me? Does she try to help me figure out what *I* want to do in my life, not what *she* thinks I should do?
- Is my potential careermate an optimistic personality who looks on the bright side of life and who believes we both can win?

If you can answer in the affirmative to most (or preferably all) of these questions, then sign her up! You want someone in this role who can really help you and not just someone you like. Think long and hard about your choice. Then take the winning candidate to a kickoff dinner! You're about to have lots of fun together.

Rachel's Assumption 5:   Rejection letters mean nobody wants you.
Flip Side: Rejection letters mean nothing.

You can pretend they mean something. You can take them personally, you can feel bad, you can tell yourself you're doomed. But all they really mean is that you just haven't found your perfect match yet. It's out there, though; you just have to keep looking.

You might dramatically improve the odds, of course, by taking to heart what we've been saying in these pages: Rely more on building career relationships than on impersonal mailings of your resumé. Rejection letters pile up only when career advancement plans emphasize those traditional techniques we so disdain.

Your likelihood of career success by mail must be calculated in light of two somewhat disheartening factors:

1. Your competition is much, much greater, since most people take this road.
2. If you have fewer face-to-face meetings, you will be judged primarily on inanimate paperwork, not on who you really are and what you can contribute.

So save a bundle on postage. Stop mailing out so many darned resumés. Search for your success in the presence of real live people.

Advancement Tools Checklist

Let's now take stock of your advancement "tools." It doesn't hurt to have a career treasure chest that's well equipped with a toolbox or repair kit to supplement all the other ideas we've offered you. Remember, it's always worked for Batman—just check out his utility belt!

In the list below, which items have you made available to yourself?

- Resumé
- Cover letter
- Access to a word processor
- Call waiting
- Answering machine
- List of career allies, including addresses and phone numbers

- Carefully chosen careermate
- Board of mentors
- Membership in relevant professional organization
- Contact with your alumni association
- Box of printed thank-you cards

How'd you do on this one? More and more these days, you hear career advancement campaigns likened to marketing plans in business. That model demands that you make it easy for customers to understand your product (you) and to be able to reach you when they want to. Thus with the first three items on this list you're creating brochure and marketing materials, including the capacity to tailor these materials to your individual customers' (potential employers') needs.

In the next item, you're providing easy access to you. Some folks object to this suggestion, however. "I hate call waiting," they say. "I don't like to get interrupted during a call." Well, we've never been prone to shill for the phone company, but we would only ask you this: If a potential employer wanted to call you to suggest you come in for an interview, would you want them to get a busy signal? Are you so confident in your chances for employment that you'd trust them to keep trying and trying if your line stayed busy? You wouldn't worry about missing such a call?

The same is true for an answering machine, though most everyone does have one these days. Remember, the Lord helps those who help themselves. Get call waiting and keep your answering machine turned on *at all times.*

We've already talked at length about the next four items on the list. We'd only add here that you should try to keep your career allies list as complete and up-to-date as possible. Again, any marketing expert worth her salt will tell you that your mailing list could be worth ten times its weight in gold. Review it, revise it, work with it. Your coming career victory will likely emerge from it.

Have you forgotten about your alumni association? If you've graduated from a college, junior college, technical/secretarial school, or even your high school, use its resources. There might be a career library there, or free career counselors, or an alumni directory available. So call them—call them right now. They've been waiting to hear from you.

Finally, there's the thank-you. Do you always remember to do this? Sure, sure, we all say we do, but do you? If your answer is yes, then let us ask you this question: When was the last time you wrote out a thank-you and mailed it off? Be honest now.

And here's a better one—when was the last time you *received* a thank-you note?

See our point? If everybody's running about mailing off so many thank-you notes to everyone else, how come you and we don't pick up more of them in our mailbox?

"But hey, Ken and Barbara, should I send a formal, typed thank-you letter or a handwritten thank-you card?"

This one's a personal decision, really. Sending a formal thank-you might help if you want to spell out once again your most impressive career attribute (as we advised you to do in your cover letter). This might make the most sense after a job interview. Just be sure you've listened closely during the interview for what your potential employer wants most to find. Then affirm in your thank-you letter what you already suggested during your interview—that you've got it!

Personally, for our money, handwritten notes fly best. They just feel more genuine to me, more sincere, more demonstrative. Tom Peters in his *The Pursuit of WOW!* apparently agrees with us: "Writing a note demonstrates a level of effort, and is permanent. Typed or handwritten? Handwritten by a country mile. A two-line, largely unreadable scrawl beats a page and a half spit out by the laser printer."

We're with ol' Tom. The more you make this game a personal one, the more likely you'll get exactly what you've come looking for.

FROM THE ADMIN FILES

Name of ex-admin: Angela Maffeo

Currently: Developing a career in psychology and writing

Admin skills used today: Organizational skills, knowing how to "read" people, typing, accounting skills, knowledge of legal issues

How change was made: "I'd spent many years early in my 'career' not seeing my work as a secretary as a career at all. To me it was just a way to make money while still spending time with my kids. I used to take jobs in September and then quit in May. I'd spend the summer with my children.

"Then one day I was sitting out by the pool in the back of our house and realized the kids weren't there anymore. They were off with their friends. So why did I have to hang around all day waiting for them? I knew then that I could start making career decisions that mattered to *me*.

"Though I returned to work as usual that fall, as a legal secretary, this time I also networked like crazy and came up with a very promising opportunity. I prepared to leave the law firm, but as I gave my notice, the firm's managing partner pushed a job description across my desk and asked if I'd be interested. It was a position as a chief administrator for a trust that managed a professional football stadium.

"This was not just a job for an admin. It required people skills, negotiating skills, accounting and budgeting skills, understanding of legal documents—a whole range of things that I'd acquired during my admin days. One of my first secretarial jobs was at a C.P.A. firm, where I learned a lot about accounting. Later, as I raised my family, I served as volunteer treasurer for the local League of Women Voters. So I'd picked up a lot of expertise along the way.

"I took the job! I really enjoyed it too. It was stimulating, challenging, personally satisfying—many of the aspects I'd missed as admin to a law firm. Today, years later, as I develop my new career in psychology, I've gone back to using my admin background to pay my bills via temp jobs, which is one of the great things about admin work—you can always get a job in it again. I'm once more focused on work that will stimulate me and on using my admin skills to help me be successful at it."

Best advice for admins: "Focus on something you care about and don't let anyone dissuade you. You're not your job; you're a human being with great potential. If your present work doesn't stimulate you, go out and find a form of work that does."

FROM THE ADMIN FILES

Name of ex-admin: Kristina Cavanaugh

Currently: Freelance paralegal, San Mateo, California

Admin skills used today: An eye for details, research skills, efficiency with paperwork, a knack for asking "the right people the right questions"

How change was made: For five years, Kristina worked as a legal secretary for a major law firm in San Francisco. She loved the atmosphere from the start, soaking up the intrigue that came with high-profile cases and the investigative challenge of legal research behind the scenes. When she talked about where she worked and what she saw around her with her family and friends, no one could deny her excitement.

"Sometimes people would wonder just what it was that I liked so much," she recalls. "Some people would ask me, wasn't it boring, all those facts to look up and details to check, and the plodding along day after day without fanfare. Other admins I knew who had worked in a legal office said that they'd found legal work too boring."

But for whatever reason, other admins' boredom proved to be Kristina's stimulation. "I loved getting up every day and going to work at the law firm," she says, "but I also knew, after a while, that I was going to need too to get involved on a much deeper level one day."

After considering law school, she instead decided to become a paralegal. It would take her faster to her goal of stretching beyond her secretary's role and give her time to consider if she wanted to move up any higher. "In some ways, being a paralegal isn't much different from being an admin—except I often work longer hours these days! I may go to law school someday, but first I want to see if I continue to enjoy this kind of work. Maybe I'm not yet confident enough that I could pass the law boards and really become a lawyer myself. It seems like such a far-off goal. Yet I get more confident every day about this work, which I can really see myself staying in my whole life."

Best advice for admins: "If you don't like the place where you work or the people you work for, leave. There are so many different kinds of work atmospheres. Find a place you like."

8

Moving On and Moving Up

There's no guarantee that anything in this book will work. There's no way of knowing for sure that you will ever achieve any of your goals within the time you allot for them. Nor can you be certain that you will achieve any of them at all. Career advancement can sometimes become a protracted battle that not everyone can win. Many in fact will give up. Others will be disappointed with how things turn out.

Still others will wage the very best campaigns imaginable, but sometimes the chips refuse to fall where they should. As the great jazz bassist Russell George once said, "Baby, they don't give it away."

But you've got to try. Without conjuring up your hopes and dreams, without valiantly expressing them to the world, without embarking on a plan of action to make them reality, nothing much tends to happen. You've simply got to fight for what you want. Sometimes you'll win and sometimes you'll lose. It's called "life."

We've found, though, that by putting goals down on paper, we can create a frame of mind that fires us to practical action. It's a mysterious cause-and-effect dynamic, not entirely explainable. But it does seem to work.

In fact, we've seen it work exactly this way many times, not only in our own lives but in the lives of our program graduates. Again and again, admins and other professionals, after making a remarkably successful career change, excitedly reported to us how they'd recently taken a glance at career goals they set for themselves while in our career program, some perhaps a year or two in the past, and how amazed they were to see how much had come true.

Though they'd stopped looking at their list of goals, stopped planning action steps, stopped reviewing their progress, they'd created enough momentum to make things happen.

One day just for fun, they glanced back at these earlier goals and took a look for nostalgic reasons. Lo and behold, they'd achieved, without even noticing it, nearly every one. Career goals, personal goals, fun goals, outrageous goals—most (or all) had come through for them. The "how" of that they sometimes couldn't even identify. They'd just gotten themselves on a "belief track" that they could accomplish great things, and great things indeed began coming their way.

Your Career Advancement Planner

In the accompanying worksheet, let's put together a structured action plan now for *you*. If possible, input this plan into your computer so that you'll be able to easily revise it as you go along.

Feel free to modify this format in any way. It's a basic framework, and you might want to add other features that might better suit you. For example, some people like to leave spaces for "intermediate" career positions that would lead them to their eventual career destination.

Andrea, an admin for an accounting firm, decided she wanted to one day become marketing director for a major company. To get there, she targeted such intermediate steps as "marketing intern," "marketing specialist," and "assistant marketing director." She felt these positions would be logical experiences to prepare her for her ultimate goal. In her planner, she added spaces for these intermediate positions and then made room for "steps" and "resources" sections beneath each one.

Be flexible, too, about deadlines. Please see them as guidelines only. Understand that unforeseen circumstances often prevail over time intentions. If a deadline can't be met, just revise it! The point of all this action planning is to keep yourself going, not to get there "on time." Time is an artificial construct.

New career direction: _____

I'd like to achieve this by: [*Insert date*] _____

Steps I Need to Take   **By:**

1. _____ _____

2. _____ _____

3. _____ _____

4. _____ _____

5. _____ _____

6. _____ _____

Resources I Need to Gather   **By:**

1. _____ _____

2. _____ _____

3. _____ _____

Some folks treat a goal or a deadline as a final report card on their commitment, their ability, or their self-worth. They'll go into a "shame spiral" if they don't do exactly what they said they'd do within the precise time frame they set for it.

Yet when all is said and done, it usually won't matter one little whit whether or not, for example, you attain your new career direction in two years or in two and a half. It's all so amazingly arbitrary! Just get yourself on that magical "belief track" that assures that yes, you're gonna do it. Then slip into the driver's seat. The fact that you're doing all you can to get there is what really matters.

Building Career Relationships—Revisited!

Not long ago, Dorothy, a savvy, aggressive executive admin, came to Barbara reeking of frustration. She'd been conducting her job search for some months now full steam ahead. She knew what she wanted, she'd been carrying out her action steps, and she'd been making connections and working on her career relationships.

"Yet I don't seem to be getting anywhere," she cried. "I think I'm doing all the right things, but I'm not getting any offers and all too few interviews."

She showed Barbara her career advancement planner. She'd added a section containing information on her career allies. Over 600 names were in it, including addresses, phone numbers, fax numbers, notes about personal interests (and foibles), information on various companies, lists of the major players—everything!

Dorothy [*flipping through the pages, looking for a magic answer*]: What am I doing wrong? I'm meeting lots of people but nothing seems to be happening.

At first glance, Dorothy did seem to be doing just as we advised her. But then Barbara started asking her questions.

Barbara: Have you had career conversations with these people over the phone or in person?

Dorothy: I speak to them first over the phone. Then if it seems to make sense I get them to meet me at their offices or over lunch. And yes, I pick up the check and mail them thank-you notes.

B.L.: When do you follow up with them after that?

Dorothy: I usually make a phone call about two or three weeks later to see if anything's come up since I last talked to them. If I don't get them in person, I leave a voice message for them. I don't want them to feel I'm pestering them.

B.L.: And when do you speak to them after that?

Dorothy [*a little taken aback at this question*]: After that?

B.L.: Yes. After your second or third contact, when do you get in touch with them again?

Dorothy: Well, I, uh, I don't.

B.L.: You don't? You stop talking with them?

Dorothy: Well, as I said, I don't want to pester them. They've learned all they can about me, and they know what I'm looking for. After two or three contacts I figure they'll let me know if they hear of anything.

Barbara reminded Dorothy of Burger King, McDonald's, and Wendy's pumping us with TV ads every evening starting around eight o'clock. She suggested that if Dorothy turned on the TV right then and there or picked up a magazine, she might also find some mention of Toyota, Jeep Eagle, Chrysler/Plymouth, or Oldsmobile.

B.L. [*laughing*]: Why do you think all these companies keep "pestering" us so much?

Dorothy [*seriously and without hesitation*]: Because they want our business. Because each one wants us to think of them first.

The moral of this little story? While it's fine to take care that you don't become a pest, you must also be careful not to stray over to the other side, where you're never heard from again, as Dorothy did. Those who advertise their wares to us ad nauseam don't want to be pests either, but they also don't want to be forgotten. They know that it's all too easy to lose us. So keep advertising—incessantly!

Listen to the words of Alan Weiss, writing in his fabulous how-to guide, *Million Dollar Consulting*: "It is actually difficult to contact clients too much. It is easy to fail to contact them frequently enough. . . . The secret is simple: Establish an ongoing dialogue with clients. In the worst case, a monologue will do."

So, as Barbara told Dorothy, by all means find ways to keep in touch. Make your ways interesting, relevant, nonthreatening, but keep them coming. If you don't, your contacts will figure you've either (1) given up your job search or (2) found what you were looking for (and thus no longer need their help).

Now this of course presumes that your contacts think about you at all. Memories fade quickly, and with so much clutter in our lives, and so much else that clamors for our attention, it's pretty easy to forget about someone we met only once or twice many moons ago.

"But hey, Barbara and Ken, how do we do this anyhow? How can we keep in touch with our contacts without pestering them?"

Heck, you want answers for everything, don't you? OK, we'll toss you a few bones:

- *Leave chatty voice messages.* Mention something relevant you heard in the news, or a good book you've just read that you think a contact would like. Don't make these messages too long (two minutes tops!), just long enough to remind them you exist. You'll of course say something like, "Just wanted to check in with you. I'm still out there searching for a position as a [*whatever*]. Let me know if you get any ideas for me. You can still call me at [*phone number*]. Thanks again for all your help. Bye for now."

- *Send contacts a copy of an article they might like.* Once you've had a good career conversation with someone, you'll know a lot about them. Are they interested in fly fishing? Management trends? Chaos theory? Madonna? Samuel Beckett?

Just send them something to read now and then with a note explaining, "Thought you might like to see this." Know what? They probably will.

- *Periodically mail out "campaign update letters."* These are kind of like a newsletter (you can even format it that way if you like) in which you let people know about your progress.

Item: "I've had three interviews this month. Two went pretty well, and I've already been called back for one."

Item: "I'm still looking for contacts at Gerard Corporation. Anybody out there know anyone who works there? Let me know!"

Item: "I've gotten more familiar with the leading customer service techniques in the retail industry. It's always fascinating to me to learn about customer service since that's what I want to do. Anybody know any good contacts in retail for me, or books or articles to read?''

It's like the board of mentors concept: You want to keep your career allies on your mailing list involved in your progress and crystal-clear about what you're looking for. Be sure to plaster your phone number all over this communiqué. It should be somewhere at least once on every page. Never assume that your phone number is easily at hand.

Have You Hugged Yourself Today?

It's easy to forget, isn't it? Some of us don't even think we deserve it. Rarely does the idea show up in a career or business book. Have you rewarded yourself today for taking on this challenge of career transition? Have you acknowledged yourself for how strong you are, how wise, how brave? Are you giving yourself the kudos you need to keep your spirits up and your confidence high?

Yes, this is part of *your* job, not just your careermate's. You've got to take time out now and then to smell the resumé paper. You've got to remind yourself why this battle is so important to you. You've got to credit yourself for taking on one of the hardest climbs in life—the excruciating baby-step-by-baby-step career hike to the stars. You're halfway up the mountain right now. Take a good look at the view. You got yourself this far. Congratulations!

Acknowledgment Mind Map

How about another mind map? We'll call this one Your Acknowledgment Mind Map. This time you'll start out with "I Acknowledge Myself For," and then proceed to do just that for all the personal progress you've made. Make your lines or tentacles represent "brave actions," "inner barriers broken," "new accomplishments," "lessons learned," and so forth.

Acknowledgment Mind Map

When you run out of great things to say about yourself, show this map to your careermate or to a friend or spouse or coworker. Ask them to share what *they* think you've done that's so impressive. As always, have a lot of fun with this map and use colored markers or crayons to make it sparkle.

Taking Direct Action

There usually comes a point during this process when you feel as though you're hitting a wall. You *know* what you want, you *know* the field you want to work in, you *know* exactly which department, division, or new company you'd like to be hired by. You can see the perfect job title under your name. And, guess what, it's *not* "administrative assistant."

When these kinds of visions begin coming your way, the time has come for—trumpets please—Direct Action!

In some cases, Direct Action will be fairly straightforward. If you've decided to go back to school, you'll call for college catalogues and begin poring over them. If you've decided to start your own business, you'll get some business counseling, perhaps secure a loan or two, formulate your business plan, and start setting up shop.

But if you've set your sights on a new employer-employee relationship, you've got to jump on any job leads you come across and generate as many new ones as you can. Remember, possibilities abound; you've just got to take the initiative to entice them your way.

Get started by examining your allies list. Who's been good for you, who's been a dud? Some on your list will be constantly feeding you great ideas, solid leads, encouragement. Place *A*'s next to those who have really helped you so far, *B*'s next to those who have only been OK, and *C*'s next to those who haven't helped much at all. Has anybody been downright discouraging, antagonistic, stupid? Place a *D* next to this joker and cross him off your list. So long, frump-face!

Now ask yourself the following questions. Scan your allies list to jog your memory if answers don't come readily to mind.

- Have any of your allies mentioned current openings, or openings that may be coming up in the future?
- Have any of your allies mentioned expanding operations or new projects in their departments (or at their companies)?
- Has anyone commented on the need for someone new to come in and solve a festering problem?
- How might any of your allies benefit from adding you to their staff, perhaps in ways they're not even aware of?

Naturally you want to keep in mind your career vision. Not every opportunity or job opening is for you. You must continually ask yourself, "Is this something I want?" Be careful of jumping onto a bandwagon just because there's an opening of some kind. You don't want to land somewhere as an admin in all but the name.

When people have been at this process for a while, if nothing's yet come through, they sometimes begin getting fidgety. They start to think, "Maybe I ought to get practical and take something I know I can do for now. I can keep looking for my dream on the side. Maybe it's not yet my time."

Bunkum! Your time is now. You're merely feeling your courage and self-confidence start to waver. That's natural, with all you've been through. So get back on your horse and ride. Remember, there's gold in them thar' hills!

Go look again at your advancement planner, your career vision, and all of your mind maps. You can do this, you really can. You can make this move.

Getting in an Ally's Face

What can you say to your allies when you know they've got something you want? How do you talk turkey with them? How do you move this process along?

Elementary, dear admin: You level with them. You get together and you speak to them very directly. You ask them for exactly what you want. You call in favors:

"Bill, as you know, I've been exploring a new career lately, and I've just completed a business course in risk analysis. The insurance field interests me more and more. I've learned a lot from what you've told me about your employer, People Mutual, and I've decided I'd love to work there. Are there any openings you know of? Is there anyone hiring you could help me meet?"

"Sarah, I've appreciated your help these past few months as I've explored my career options. I'm now certain that marketing is my future. What could I do to become a part of your department? I'd really be excited to work for you."

"Beth, I get more and more enthralled with everything I learn about the restaurant business. I've decided what I'd most like to do is manage. Do you know of any assistant management positions at any establishments in town? I realize you have nothing to offer me yourself right now, but anything else you've heard of that might get me started would be great."

Don't try to copy down these speeches verbatim. They're designed just to give you the basic idea. You want to say what's on your mind in as natural a tone as possible, but you don't want to demand. You're just continuing to lead your allies in a way that helps you. You need something specific from them now, and you have to communicate that.

Taking this more direct approach now moves you into a more assertive phase in your climb out of the pink-collar ghetto. By now, if you've done your homework, you've established solid relationships in the new career area of your choice. Given that, you'll find many allies delighted that you're asking for help. Some may even have been wondering when you'd get around to it. Just remember that it's always your job to make known what you want, and to articulate to your allies how they can help you attain it.

The Dread Job Interview

Once you begin taking Direct Action, you'll also begin hearing about specific opportunities. At some point you'll advance to the formal step of job interviewing and doing whatever else it takes to capitalize on an opportunity.

But excuse us, did we hear you gasp a little when we mentioned interviewing? What's that? You say you'd rather wrap your hand around a red-hot poker? Oh, come on now, you can't be serious. Things couldn't be that bad.

Yet of course for many of us (most of us?), it is. The fear comes from worrying about getting it "right"—fielding tough interview questions, spitting back perfect answers, holding on to your cool while questions come flying at you left and right. It's like sharing tea and crumpets with John Houseman.

Keep this in mind, then: You don't have to get it "right," you just have to be yourself. Sounds too simple, doesn't it? Yet it's true.

We're not saying you don't have to prepare, or think out your answers, or phrase what you say in terms that emphasize your strengths. It's just that, despite all of this, that indefinable connection, the chemistry between you and the interviewer, that mysterious "something" in the air will have as much to do with any final decision as all of your "perfect" answers put together.

We're forever asking audiences what criteria they've used in the past to hire someone. We get the same answers every time:

"It's a gut decision."
"Whether the candidate can fit in with the culture."
"How well I think we'll get along."
"Chemistry."
"The candidate's enthusiasm."

You've already convinced the interviewer that you're qualified (otherwise, why would he have arranged this interview?). Next, as with resumés, your interview should not throw your potential employer a curve ball. It should confirm everything the employer has come to believe about you up to now. If you just answer questions to the best of your ability, your store of knowledge, experience, and creativity should nestle you through.

But you can't fabricate chemistry. It's either going to be there or it's not. Because of this, you can't really "fail." If you generate enough job interviews, the right chemistry will materialize with someone. Your "perfect match" is out there waiting.

This natural chemistry is obviously what you most want to find. Otherwise, that new work environment with you in it won't be fun for anyone. Including you.

Our overall advice is this: The best job interview is a good career conversation. That's your umbrella. You want your interview, after all, to be, as Rick (Humphrey Bogart) suggests to Louis at the end of *Casablanca*, "the beginning of a beautiful friendship." You want it to assume the lofty position of Supreme Career Relationship for at least the next few years. It's the beginning of a long-running dialogue.

"But hey, Ken and Barbara, how do I do this? It's an interview, after all, and I'm not in control. My job is to shut up and answer their questions."

That's the way you may have been taught to think of interviews, yes, but that's your "factory mentality" showing through. Again, put yourself in the driver's seat. Shift the process around so it serves your needs.

Interview Hint 1: Chat When You First Walk In

You'd be surprised how often we're told by employers that this doesn't happen. People enter stiff, scared, subservient. They don't act like themselves. Especially admins.

Break down your inner barriers! You're not back at your workstation or the reception desk now. You don't have to just shut up and follow orders. You're an adult. You're a person. Be friendly; comment on the weather or how nice a building it is or the route you took to get there. As long as you're not obnoxious, critical, or negative, it really doesn't matter what you say. You're just trying to break the ice and set a tone that you've come to interact, not just slavishly answer questions.

But note: Don't let yourself be the only one chatting. While you'll want to chat a bit when you first come in, lord knows you don't want to run off at the mouth. Chatting is a two-way street: Let the person you're meeting slip in a few words as well. Watch where he goes with his comments and follow the conversation where he takes it.

Anything you hear now could be a clue to how the interviewer thinks, what he's looking for, how you could help his company. Keep chatting, but let him slowly begin doing more chatting than you. Listen closely to what he has to say. This bears repeating: *Listen closely!*

Interview Hint 2: Realize That Your Interviewer May Be Just as Nervous as You

Many interviewers, believe it or not, don't have the slightest idea how to conduct an interview. They fumble with your resumé, ask stilted, "textbook" questions, and struggle to jot down your answers. Eccchhh! Who needs this?

Ease your interviewer's mind, have pity on him. Subtly convert the interview into a career conversation. If you get your interviewer to feel relaxed and enjoying himself by the end of your session, you've accomplished what you came for. He'll like you.

Interview Hint 3: Observe the "20/2 Rule"

When answering questions, keep them longer than twenty seconds but under two minutes. Too short an answer conveys the impression that the speaker has little to offer, and too long an answer evokes the image of a boorish windbag who lives for the spotlight.

Even yes or no questions should be elaborated upon. Like other questions, they're opportunities to expand your case. Let's look first at the wrong way to do it, as exemplified by Candidate 1:

The Wrong Way

Interviewer: I see by your resumé you went to Duke University.
Candidate 1: Yap.

Interviewer: Did you like it there?

Candidate 1: Yap.

Interviewer: You graduated with honors, third in your class—that's impressive.

Candidate 1: Thanks.

Interviewer: Anything you'd like to add that we haven't covered?

Candidate 1: Nope.

Wow! What electricity, excitement! You can almost imagine an interviewer jumping up and down, shouting, "I love your simplicity! When can you start?"

Now compare that scenario with this unarguably more effective one:

The Right Way

Interviewer: I see by your resumé you went to Duke University.

Candidate 2: Sure did. It wasn't my first choice back in high school, but it turned out to be the right place for me. I'd thought I'd prefer a smaller school closer to home—I'm from Wyoming—but as it turned out, the many opportunities at a major school gave me, I believe, a richer education.

Interviewer: So you liked it there?

Candidate 2: Oh yes. I think that's where I first began enjoying scientific research, in fact. Though I studied a straight business curriculum, they always had major science exhibits going on there. I was fascinated with them. That's why this position as a scientific research assistant appeals to me so much.

Interviewer: I see too that you graduated with honors, third in your class. *Impressive.*

Candidate 2: Thank you. I studied pretty hard there. I always felt my education was an opportunity to grow, not just pick up a diploma. So I threw myself into my studies. I took my commitment to my workload pretty seriously.

What do you think? Whom would you prefer—Candidate 1 or Candidate 2? Obviously, by adding her charm and responsiveness to her impressive credentials, Candidate 2 clearly makes a strong showing. Elaborating upon what could have been simple yes or no answers, she identifies herself as: (1) curious and eager to learn, (2) interested specifically in scientific research, and (3) a hard worker. Not a bad set of attributes for the person who'll fill this job.

Interview Hint 4: Ask Questions

Interviews, by definition, tend to be one-sided. One person (job interviewer, reporter, pollster) asks questions of another, and the other responds. That's pretty much the way it's supposed to go. That's one reason both of us disdain informational interviews.

But a conversation works differently, doesn't it? Both parties ask questions, both answer questions, both make expansive comments. There's a give-and-take, there's an equal exchange. A relationship forms.

You want to create that here—a career conversation. That means you've got to throw in some questions of your own. On a very, very discreet level, you've got to alter the format.

Here's how you do it: Sometime after the interview gets started—maybe five or ten minutes, probably no longer than fifteen (use your intuition)—slip in a question at the end of one of your answers. Make this question as spontaneous as you can. Let it spring from something that's come up during the interview. For example:

Interviewer: Tell me, Melissa, what makes you feel especially qualified for this position of scientific research assistant?

Melissa: Well, I'm a pretty organized person and I can see that you'd have to be organized to keep these research data in order. Which brings up a question I've wanted to ask you: How closely would I be involved in the actual experiments themselves? I'd love to work directly in the lab at some point. Would that fit in with this position?

Notice how Melissa slides the question into the interview naturally. It is an honest thing to ask. It's worth asking simply to understand more about how things work. It also helps communicate where Melissa wants to go in her professional development.

Now the interview can move in a whole new direction. It can become more of a conversation. If the interviewer spends even a few minutes responding to Melissa's question, a tone has been set that allows for a free-flowing give-and-take. They begin a career relationship.

Interview Hint 5: Paint the Future, Not the Past

When making a case for yourself, don't dwell on jobs, functions, and achievements in your past. Explain how transferable your demonstrated skills and your accomplishments can be to a new situation. Begin leaving your admin life behind.

Go back to Melissa's assessment of herself. She called herself "a pretty organized person" rather than focusing on her admin organizational duties, such as filing, keeping her boss's calendar, sorting out mail. She then related it to her possible future—working in the research institute, organizing scientific data.

Face forward. You will most effectively make the transition into a new career area if you can literally see yourself working there. That means employing talents, skills, and abilities in the service of your new career. Once you've got that much in your sights, all you need do next is describe it for someone who can help.

Is This a Better Deal?

A day will come when you finally get a job offer that's not admin or secretarial work. It really will. So go ahead and shout "Glory hallelujah! Someone wants me, someone wants me!"

At that moment, though, you face a new question: Should you take it?

Go back to your career vision. Does this offer represent what you've been looking for? Is it the right job for you? How's the compensation? Does this position lead you anywhere?

Take a day or two to think about it. No matter how much you want a new situation, it's always good policy to sleep on it. You might be missing something, forgetting something.

When you call the next day, be diplomatic, courteous, respectful, enthusiastic, positive. But ask for something more. Maybe it's more money, a longer vacation, an upgrading in authority or responsibility. The worst they can tell you is, "We can't do that." At least you'll have tried. Most times you'll win on at least a few points.

"But hey, Barbara and Ken, I hate playing games. I'm just not comfortable with that."

It's already a game. Your potential employer more than likely expects you to come back with a request for more. They've probably factored that in. "If she asks for $2,000 more per year, let's offer her $500. If she won't accept that, we'll go to $750; $800 is our ceiling."

If you refuse to play any games at all, your discomfort may cost you a lot of money. Or more time off, or a job more to your liking. So at least play a *little* game.

How do you ask without alienating everybody? Just be careful with your language. Don't say, "You gotta gimme this. It's mine and I deserve it." Be diplomatic: "What could we do to make this work for both of us? Your figure of $34,000 feels a little low to me. I was really hoping for $40,000. What can we do to get closer to that amount?"

At some point, after playing around with the areas you'd like to see "improved," you'll get a feeling in your gut that it's time to say yes. When that moment comes, tell your new employer you're glad to be aboard. "I think we're all set," you say. "I feel great about our agreement. I'm looking forward to working with you."

Yahoo! Pop open the Dom Perignon. You've just made your new employer happy. And you've finally freed yourself from the pink-collar ghetto.

FROM THE ADMIN FILES

Name of ex-admin: Jessica Lefcourt

Currently: Web Page developer, International Links, Glenview, Illinois

Admin skills used today: Computer proficiency, phone skills, understanding of technology

How change was made: "The most fascinating aspect of my admin and secretarial years had always been learning about software and new technology. I pushed constantly to be sent to computer courses and seminars, and I loved picking up new tricks there to use in my work.

"One day, my boss called me in for a meeting. I assumed he was just going to give me a list of things he needed done in the coming week. Instead, he floored me with what he had to say. 'A lot of people in the company are pretty impressed with your work,' he began. 'I'm not just talking about your regular duties but all that you've learned on the computer. We've really come to rely on your advice and know-how.'

"I thanked him for the compliments. I thought maybe he was going to give me a little raise.

" 'We're going to be opening up a new division, serving customers who want to get on the Internet,' he continued. 'We want you to be part of it.'

"Again, naturally I assumed he meant I'd work there as an admin. But it turned out that people had started literally turning to me for advice about technical matters. I'd become an in-house expert. So I was being elevated from admin to technical developer. My job would be to work closely with our customers and create advertisements for them over the Internet, specifically the World Wide Web.

" 'Congratulations,' my boss concluded, reaching out to shake my hand. 'I'm going to hate to lose you but you're really needed in this new department. You're a pretty valuable person around here.' "

"Yes, I got a raise too—a big one!"

Best advice for admins: "Learn as much as you can about all you do and become a real expert. There are new products and services developing all the time. You can step into something new if you've got something special to offer."

FROM THE ADMIN FILES

Name of ex-admin: Judy Wagner

Currently: Counseling assistant for Kathleen Greer Associates, a Framingham, Massachusetts, provider of employee assistance programs (EAPs).

Admin skills used today: Organizational and scheduling skills, meeting-planning skills, "intuitive hearing," that is, the ability to perceive why people are calling and to identify their true agenda

How change was made: "I was working as an admin for a nonprofit agency where my present boss, Kathy Greer, had been renting an office. Part of my position was to answer her phones too. She was impressed with the quality of my work and crisis intervention hotline training. So when she was ready to hire her first admin, she asked me if I'd be interested.

"I might not have taken the job except that what she was offering me was more than the typical admin position. As a provider of EAP services, Kathy needed someone who could be sensitive to anyone who called. Often a call to an EAP is a cry for help. With emotional issues or with some kind of addiction, callers need to feel comfortable about calling. It also might be necessary to do some crisis intervention counseling.

"Kathy wanted me to help with arranging seminars and scheduling her staff too. She was in effect offering me the chance to use both parts of what I do best—organizational skills *and* my ability to hear what's really being said when someone calls. She also offered me a four-day work week, which may have been the clincher! I had wanted to reduce my work schedule for a long time."

Best advice for admins: "Follow your interests. You're likely to do well in things you're most interested in—and get the most satisfaction from them too. Be professional. That means having a positive attitude and a willingness to learn. Stay away from gossip mills and company politics."

9

Settling In to New Digs

So here you are, at your new desk in your new office. Your window looks out on the city below, and you have a door you can close. You've even got the services of—gasp!—an admin to help you out! (You share her with three others, but that's all right.)

You begin fixing up your office the way you like: a little vase with flowers you picked up on the way to work, pictures of your loved ones, your favorite paperweight, a cute, tiny clock. As you fuss about, you smile to yourself, remembering: "I've worked very hard to get myself here. I've escaped the pink-collar ghetto."

Suddenly, you hear someone outside distinctly cry out for coffee. Without thinking, you leap to your feet and begin bustling toward your office door. You run to get it even though you're not sure where it is.

"Two creams," the man barks. "No sugar."

You're almost out your door when you stop dead in your tracks. What in the heck are you doing? You're fetching someone's coffee? Don't you get it? That's no longer your job!

Sweeter thoughts never crossed your mind. You turn back and take a good, hard look at your new office. This may take some getting used to. You've been fetching coffee and screening calls and correcting typos for so long, you're conditioned to jump when somebody—anybody!—calls for you.

You realize it's time for a few attitude changes.

Nurturing a New Professional Self-Image

Do you really see yourself yet as a professional on a level beyond that of an admin? Can you see it, feel it? Do you believe it?

If you're having trouble with this at all, create a pack of what we'll call "New-Image Cards," as shown in Figure 9-1. Get a stack of index cards and deal out about fifteen or twenty. On each card, write out a statement that expresses something about the new you. Make each statement affirmative, active, dynamic. Make it also something you haven't quite grasped yet, that you're not yet sure you truly believe.

But make it something you absolutely *want* to believe.

Once you've put together your New-Image Cards, keep them with you all day. From time to time yank them out and shuffle through them. Read each carefully, sensing how strongly (or how little) you believe what it says.

At first, you'll not sense a real connection with any of the cards. You'll feel as though they're talking about someone else. But remember: They're designed to help you acquire a new image, not to reinforce the one you already have. They're describing a you in the making.

As you read through your cards time after time after time, day after day, you'll begin reprogramming your mind. Some of the cards' statements will begin getting inside of you. They'll work their subtle magic on your inner barriers, so that one day you'll pick up a card, read it, then matter-of-factly think, "Well, yes, that's true." When that happens, throw the card out! Replace it with a new one! Your new card's statement will then express another belief about yourself you haven't adopted yet.

It's important to see your first post–admin position as a step forward for your new self, and to begin discarding—or at least taking control of—old beliefs that can no longer serve you. As the title of Peter McWilliam's book states, *You Can't Afford the Luxury of a Negative Thought*. Get in the habit of positive thinking.

Tooting Your Own Horn

You've apparently been doing this pretty well. After all, it was central to your career advancement campaign, which got you

Figure 9-1. New-Image Cards

here. And though advertising yourself may not have been the most comfortable fit at first, we're sure that by now you've gotten at least a little more used to it. In your new work environment, however, you've got to take it up a thousand notches.

See all those busy beavers scurrying around outside your new office? How many of them have you gotten to know yet? We don't mean you've been casually introduced. We mean, how many have you *really* gotten to know?

That's precisely what you have to do. You can't wait for people to approach you—that's Old Work World stuff. This time you have to approach them. You want them to know who you are, what you've been hired to do, and that your goal is to be there for *them.*

You want them to think of you as a true team player. You want to make a difference big-time to your new "family." So you'll invite each of them to have lunch with you. (And yes, you'll still lunge for that tab!) In the process of getting to know them, you're continuing your career advancement by initiating career conversations and further building career relationships. This never ends.

Seeking Out Feedback

You probably got a lot of feedback as an admin. Most of it was probably after the fact. Especially the negative.

With things always frantic, chaotic, charged, what you usually learned from this feedback probably amounted to very little. You could never learn much from your mistakes because everything came and went in a blur. But that's your life as an admin. "Quoth the Raven, 'Nevermore.'"

In your new professional life, you'll seek out feedback; you'll relish it. That's right, you'll look for it, uncover it, ask to have it delivered to your door. In your new position you can't afford to let your mistakes go uncorrected or your bad habits fester. You need to be on top of things.

How can you be sure that you develop steadily this time, that you grow professionally, and that you incorporate "unsuccessful experiments" (failures, mistakes, errors) into a learning curve that makes you better? Paul Falcone told us that asking your new boss for periodic performance reviews throughout the year would be one way to do it. As Falcone explains in his book:

> By asking your boss for quarterly or even monthly per-
> formance updates, you'll show yourself as someone
> looking for ways to improve [her]self, an individual
> open to constructive criticism, and a person with out-
> standing communication skills. Most significantly,
> you'll get a steady stream of feedback that will help
> you improve your performance. That way, when it
> comes time for the annual performance appraisal,
> you'll have had a head start on gathering the informa-
> tion necessary to have fixed most of the weaker issues
> in advance! This is a winning strategy for a well-in-
> formed, career-conscious, information-hungry em-
> ployee geared for career progression.

Wise words. Speak to your new boss about frequent performance reviews today.

Piping Up at Staff Meetings

Maybe you did a lot of this as an admin, although most admins report they don't. It doesn't feel like their place, they say. They don't often feel a part of the team.

Well, you're a part of the team now! Speak your piece. Inject an idea or a question here and there. Let people hear what's on your mind.

It's a good idea, however, to *listen* too, especially in your first few weeks. Make sure you don't rush in too fast with too many fabulous new opinions. People will accept you more readily in the early days if you don't act like you know every-thing before you've had a chance to know much of anything.

Bide your time: Take a lot in, hear people's ideas, observe the group dynamics in your new department or at company staff meetings. After you've got the lay of the land, see to it that you position yourself as a major player. You've been hired to be fully involved. Stay that way.

Note of caution: For your new relationships to gel effectively, you have to locate a common ground. That happens best when you really listen to another and try to absorb what that other is saying. Always keep listening. It's called team spirit.

Setting Boundaries

As an admin you may not have always felt comfortable saying no to your boss when he'd dump a piping-hot stack of documents on your desk at ten minutes to five, muttering, "I'll need these in the computer by eight tomorrow morning. Have a nice night." You may never have set many boundaries around how much work is reasonable or how much might be going over the line.

But if you've never learned to set limits before, you definitely have to learn to set them now. If you don't, you'll slowly revert to adminship all over again. You're working in a fast, pressure-cooker work world these days—that's something you already know, we realize—in which some people will take advantage. They may take advantage without realizing it, but take advantage, nonetheless, they will. That's why it's up to you to set boundaries. No one else will step in and do it for you.

The following scenarios represent stepping-over-the-boundaries dilemmas you might find yourself faced with in your new position. Think for a moment about what you should do if any of these situations comes storming your way.

DILEMMA 1

One of Belinda's new colleagues, John, asks her to take over a "minor" project he's been having trouble with. "You know a lot more about this than I do, Belinda," he says. "Maybe you could work it through for me?"

Belinda knows she's got a lot on her plate right now. How can she tactfully deflect John's request?

Make a few notes here summarizing your thoughts:

_____

_____

_____

_____

_____

Dilemma 2

Helena's boss, Mark, drops a heavy assignment into her in-basket. He's marked it ASAP on a Post-it. Helena remembers this same problem, time and time again, from her previous admin job. She's already rushing to finish another assignment he's given her, due by the end of the week. Which is more important?

How can Helena know when Mark truly needs the new assignment and how much priority he's ascribed to the first assignment?

Make a few notes here summarizing your thoughts:

_____

_____

_____

_____

_____

Dilemma 3

Marguerite's new boss, Mr. Hightower, invites her and her husband, Jim, to dinner on Saturday night at his house. But it's the third time in the last two months, and Marguerite has begun to feel enough is enough. Jim's not too pleased either. What should she tell Mr. Hightower?

Make a few notes here summarizing your thoughts:

_____

_____

_____

_____

_____

DILEMMA 4

Some new colleagues of Lisa's meet every Thursday for lunch. Lisa quickly sees that all that ever seems to go on at these luncheons is office gossip, snippy comments, and cynical remarks.

Lisa's joined them three times already but doesn't want to continue. What can she do or say?

Make a few notes here summarizing your thoughts:

_____

_____

_____

_____

_____

There are an infinite number of responses that any of us could come up with for these scenarios. Don't look at your answers as a right-wrong thing. Whatever works, especially in touchy situations, can be deemed correct.

All your responses should be based on an essential need to remain sensitive, tactful, respectful. You don't want to start alienating the same folks you're trying to win over. So don't get angry; get resourceful instead. Choose your words and reactions with care. Here are some responses we feel meet those criteria:

Response to Dilemma 1: "I'd like to help, John, I really would, but honestly I can't fit anything new in right now." Belinda thinks a moment. "But what I could do is take a few minutes and help you figure out how you could best handle this. I do have a little more experience here, so maybe I can act as your 'consultant.' Why don't we sit down at lunchtime and talk about steps you could take to get you through this."

Response to Dilemma 2: Helena should ask for guidelines straight out. "I can get right on this new assignment, if that's what you want," Helena tells Mark. "But I have a question for you: Should I drop this other assignment I've been working on?

When you say ASAP, when exactly do you mean? What's your absolute deadline for each of these assignments?"

Response to Dilemma 3: "Mr. Hightower, would you mind if Jim and I passed on your kind invitation this Saturday? We've enjoyed dinner with you and Mrs. Hightower in the past, but lately we feel we haven't been spending as much time at home as we'd like. For the time being, we've decided to cut down on our social events and just spend more time with each other."

Additional advice: If Mr. Hightower doesn't take the hint and his invitations persist, then a heart-to-heart talk may be in order. Is Mr. Hightower the kind of person an employee can talk to frankly? Has he shown himself to be open to other points of view? If so, Marguerite should tell him that, in her experience, when boundaries between work and personal life get too ambiguous, they make relationships at work confusing and ambiguous too. Bosses may start having trouble telling their "employee-friends" what to do; employees have trouble allowing their "boss-friend" sufficient authority. Maybe there's an experience from Marguerite's past or an experience of a friend of hers she could relate to Mr. Hightower.

In any event, this approach, when it works, will also avoid future cat-and-mouse games with an overly chummy boss. It takes a little more courage to raise an issue like this face-to-face, but the payoff could be longer lasting.

Response to Dilemma 4: Lisa should put her colleagues off by eating lunch at her desk, or saying, "I have so much to do, I'm working through lunch today." She should also start making plans to meet other folks for lunch. Though her "old buddies" may start gossiping about her, once she begins avoiding them, at least she'll be free.

Additional advice to Lisa: Don't waste a moment of your precious workday on things that won't advance you, or that are petty or mean-spirited. Get away from those folks as fast as your legs can carry you. That's right, you heard us: *Run!*

Sliding Back Down the Chute

You don't want to fall backward. You don't want to unconsciously step onto a trapdoor and drop back down to where you came from. You don't want to ever return to the pink-collar ghetto.

Keeping yourself from sliding back down the big chute that you've just baby-stepped your way out of may take lots of stamina. You'll also need to stay alert and in shape. Here are a few tips to maintain your "career fitness":

1. *No more hanging out in the admin pool.* This might seem pretty obvious, but it's easy to slip back into. Some ex-admins want to stay loyal, or might have friends still there or might just be waxing nostalgic. Whatever the motive, don't do it. You've got new friends now, new colleagues, new bridges to cross. Get on with it. You're not an admin any longer, you're an ex-admin. Act like one.

2. *Don't be afraid of seeming stupid.* You have to ask questions. You have to admit you're in the dark about a lot of things. You have to understand your new projects and assignments. You have to get new procedures explained to you.

When you act too smart, you may not learn what you need to know. Listen to what your colleagues are saying. When you don't understand something, ask them to explain it again. You might take a colleague aside and ask her to explain it at a later time rather than take time up at a staff meeting or with others. But one way or another, find out what you need to know. You'll get genuinely knowledgeable about things in no time.

3. *Look forward to your next career.* Does this sound premature? Maybe, but time keeps marching along. Because we can no longer count on security in today's workplace, we've got to be ever vigilant, growing, evolving. Why wait until someone X'es you off a list and you suddenly lose a great job you worked so hard to get? Don't you want to keep your career life vibrant, prosperous, meaningful, and fun?

The other incentive for thinking about your next position now is that we all change over time. What meant everything to us five years ago might mean nothing at all to us today. Continuing your career advancement campaign allows you to live, and to live well. So keep your career conversations going and your career dreams flowing!

Post–Admin Career Advancement Checklist

Using the accompanying worksheet, check off how many career advancement items you've remembered to attend to since getting hired for this post–admin position. If you find any items you can't answer with a yes or a no, then you've identified some work ahead of you. Don't wait too long to get going on any of this. Time, as we've mentioned, marches on.

	Yes	*No*
I've notified all my career allies of my new position. In my notification I've thanked them sincerely for all their assistance and good wishes.	_____	_____
Since starting my new job, I've added many new names to my career allies list.	_____	_____
I've joined a professional organization that represents my new position.	_____	_____
I've volunteered for a committee in my professional organization. I plan to stay very active.	_____	_____
I've begun subscribing to at least two professional magazines relevant to my new position.	_____	_____
I've begun looking for a new mentor. I have approached my new boss about the idea.	_____	_____
I've revised my career vision and I've worked out a timetable for achieving my *next* new career direction.	_____	_____
I've set goals for my personal life. I have also set down a timetable for achieving these goals.	_____	_____

I've redoubled my efforts to acknowledge
myself for my talents, skills, and achievements.
I reward myself for my courage and
determination every day.   _____   _____

Did You Make a Mistake?

We all make them—mistakes, that is. Sometimes we even make
a whopper. So consider this: What would you do if after, say, a
month or two at your new job, you began to feel it wasn't for
you, that taking it had been a big, big mistake?

The first things to ask yourself are: "Do I miss admin work?
Was I happier there? Was my idea of leaving admin life just a
case of the grass looking greener somewhere else?" If you've
answered no to those questions, then maybe the problem is that
you've chosen the wrong company, the wrong department, even
the wrong career. Maybe you need to rethink your new career
direction: You may simply be still in process, still looking for
that new career direction that's right for you.

The first thing to remember is: Don't panic! You can handle
this; you can get yourself to a new place. You know you can do
this because, quite simply, you just did it!

Second thing to remember: It's OK to leave. If you want to
quit, and if you can afford to, just do it. Take off, give your notice, take a hike—just get out of there! Do what you need to do.
Set yourself free.

If you have learned anything at all during this process, it
should be that you're very powerful. You weren't born an admin,
and you've proved to the world you don't have to remain one.
You found out about lots of new career possibilities, and you
took yourself down the road to at least one of them. You're a
winner now, even if your battles are still not over. (They never
are anyway, for any of us, until you-know-what.)

Back to Square One. That's right, all the way back; do not
pass Go, and get your hands off that $200.

It's not really Square One, of course. It's at least Square Two,
Three, or Four. Remember, you're not starting out as an admin
this time. Take a deep breath and believe that the next career

direction will be the one you really want. Then start thinking again about which one that will be.

FROM THE ADMIN FILES

Name of ex-admin: Rusty Stieff

Currently: Vice president in the nonprofit lending group at a major commercial bank, acting as liaison with the bank's customers in order to provide them with new services

Admin skills used today: Typing; personal organizational skills

How change was made: "I had trouble getting a job when I graduated from college in the early seventies so I went to Katy Gibbs for three months and learned secretarial skills. I ended up getting a job with the ex-mayor of Boston, the late John Collins, who worked then as an urban professor at the Sloan School of Management. I didn't do a heck of a lot with him—drove him around to places and typed a few letters. I never thought I'd stay forever as someone's personal secretary.

"I began thinking I needed to do something more professional and enrolled in a master's program at Simmons College. At some point I applied for a job at one of MIT's libraries. Right away I was told I was nuts because the pay for a library associate was actually lower than I was making by then as a secretary. 'You'd be crazy to take this job,' the HR manager told me. 'You'll be making less money.'

"Well, I guess I was crazy because I couldn't see staying in a job that didn't make me happy just for slightly more money. So eventually I got hired by the library and never went back to admin work. I've gone on from there through a series of career changes culminating in where I am now, in banking. For me, admin work was just a way to get started."

Best advice for admins: "Start taking some initiative to get what you want. I think of that old joke about the guy who wants desperately to become a doctor and keeps praying feverishly every night, getting more and more exasperated: 'Please, Lord, oh Lord, I've been so good in my life, I've observed all the commandments, I've tried to stay pure of heart. Why oh why Lord can't I become a doctor? What do I have to do?'

"One night God couldn't take it anymore. The heavens parted and His voice thundered downward. 'Apply to medical school,' he boomed.

"Admins can be like that. They've got to take concrete steps by talking to as many people as possible about fields they might be interested in. Find out what you want to do."

FROM THE ADMIN FILES

Name of ex-admin: Sophia Snow

Currently: Academic counselor at Harvard University's Extension School, counseling students on career and academic issues

Admin skills used today: "In my case, counseling skills. In one of my early jobs at the Harvard student accounts office, I counseled students about the reality of their financial situations. I'd typically say, 'Here is the amount you owe.'

"Then I moved to the financial aid office, where I could open things up a little by counseling students on how they could get the money they needed. Now I work with broader life questions where I ask, 'How would you like your life to be?'

"Each job was a stepping-stone for improving my counseling skills."

How change was made: "At the age of twelve, I read a book on Freud and thought, 'This is it! This is what I want to do.' But I also got started in admin work around the same time by working as an 'office boy' in the architectural firm where my father worked.

"When I got to Harvard, I began to meet people in other departments through routine communication required by my job. People got to know me and could see the kind of work I could do. I began to observe other people doing other jobs and I'd think, 'That department looks interesting. I might like to work over there.'

"By the time my present job opened up, I knew enough people here for them to have a good sense about my skill set. A particularly important one, I think, was knowing how to hold a student's hand, which they needed. I had definitely gotten good at this, so it seemed like a perfect match."

Best advice for admins: "Start talking about your ambitions, about where you'd rather be. Get everyone to catch your enthusiasm. Even the most unsupportive boss may start helping an admin out if she's enthusiastic. Keep thinking about what you want to do and keep your eyes and ears open. The moment I decided I wanted something else, it seemed, the information I needed came flowing my way.''

Epilogue

A well-known quote from W. H. Murray, the Scottish explorer who trekked through previously untouched regions of the Himalayas, describes a spirit of will you're going to need to make the ideas throughout this book come true for you. It goes like this:

> Until one is committed, there is hesitancy, the chance to draw back, always ineffectiveness. Concerning all acts of initiative (and creation) there is one elementary truth, the ignorance of which kills countless ideas and splendid plans: that the moment one definitely commits oneself, then Providence moves too.
>
> All sorts of things occur to help one that would never otherwise have occurred. A whole stream of events issues from the decision, raising in one's favor all manner of unforeseen incidents and meetings and material assistance, which no man could have dreamed would have come his way.
>
> I have learned a deep respect for one of Goethe's couplets: "Whatever you can do, or dream you can, begin it. Boldness has genius, power and magic in it."

That's really the way it is. You can meet this challenge—you really can. You can change your career life; you can escape the pink-collar ghetto. You've always been so much more than "just an admin."

See you at the top.

RESOURCES

Falcone, Paul. *The Complete Job-Finding Guide for Secretaries and Administrative Support Staff.* New York: AMACOM, 1995.

Gellerman, Saul W. *Motivation in the Real World.* New York: Penguin Books, 1992.

Halper, Jan. *Quiet Desperation: The Truth About Successful Men.* New York: Warner Books, 1988.

Jeffers, Susan. *Feel the Fear and Do It Anyway.* New York: Fawcett Columbine, 1987.

Koller, Alice. *The Stations of Solitude.* New York: Bantam Books, 1990.

Koltnow, Emily, and Lynne S. Dumas. *Congratulations! You've Been Fired.* New York: Fawcett Columbine, 1990.

LaRouche, Janice, and Regina Ryan. *Janice LaRouche's Strategies for Women at Work.* New York: Avon, 1984.

Prince, George M. *The Practice of Creativity.* New York: Macmillan, 1970.

Schenkel, Susan. *Giving Away Success: Why Women Get Stuck and What to Do About It.* New York: McGraw-Hill, 1984.

Seligman, Martin. *Learned Optimism.* New York: Knopf, 1990.

Seuss, Dr. *Oh, the Places You'll Go!* New York: Random House, 1990.

Stroman, J., and K. Wilson, ed. Susan Heyboer O'Keefe. *Administrative Assistant's and Secretary's Handbook.* New York: AMACOM, 1995.

Sutch, Debra. *Beyond Secretary: The Growing Role of the Administrative Assistant.* Boulder, Colo.: CareerTrack Publications, 1993 (audio program).

Weiss, Alan. *Million Dollar Consulting.* New York: McGraw-Hill, 1992.

Index